Be patient, God isn't finished with me yet.

HUMANS
IN
TRAINING

HUMANS IN TRAINING

*Everything you need
you already have...*

**you must simply learn how to use
what has already been created within**

Jay D. Allen

PUBLISHING

Toronto, Canada

PUBLISHING

Published in 2003 by HIT Publishing

Inspirational Photos: Keith Allen, *www.keithallenfineartphotography.com*
Logo: Adiction Media
Design: Heidy Lawrance Associates

National Library of Canada Cataloguing in Publication Data
Canadian Cataloguing in Publication Data
Allen, Jay D., 1969–
    Humans in training : an owner's manual

ISBN 0-9689693-1-3

1. Success in business.   2. Business ethics.   I. Title

HF5387.A59 2002   650.1   C2001-903364-8

The author is grateful for permission to include the following previously copyrighted material: 1) **Autobiography in Five Short Chapters**, Copyright ©1993 by Portia Nelson, from the book *There's A Hole In My Sidewalk*, Beyond Words Publishing, Inc., Hillsboro, Oregon, U.S.A.; 2) **The Daffodil Principle**, reprinted and adapted with the permission Atria Books, an imprint of Simon & Schuster Adult Publishing Group, from *Things I Wish I'd Known Sooner* : Personal Discoveries of a Mother of Twelve by Jaroldeen Edwards. Copyright ©1997 by Jaroldeen Edwards. Published in hardcover as *Windows of Light*.; 3) **Our Deepest Fear**, Copyright ©1992 by Marianne Williamson, from the book *A Return to Love*, reprinted by permission of HarperCollins Publishers Inc.

All effort has been made to ensure accuracy of quotes. Should there be an error, please contact us at *www.humansintraining.com* for correction in future editions.

Printed in Canada

I dedicate this book to my parents,
Keith and Mary Ellen,
for their love, patience, and support.
Dad, you are an inspiration and a great friend.
Mom, it is a privilege to know
an angel right here on earth!

Thank you both for always believing in me
and always being there.

Acknowledgments

There are many people to thank who have played a part in making this book come alive.

First, I would like to thank my family—my parents, Keith and Mary Ellen; my sisters, Jennifer and Wendy; and my nieces and nephews—Alyssa, Alexandra, Trevor, Aidan, and Erin—for being in my life. I am very fortunate to have such a loving family.

I would like to thank Shelby Hacala and Margo Fletcher. You are wonderful friends and people.

A very special thank-you to Denise McKillop for your dedication and friendship. Also I would like to thank Grace Tran, Andrea Lemieux, Simone Gabbay and Heidy Lawrance for believing in me and the Humans In Training message. And finally, I thank all those individuals whom I have had the privilege of meeting through my seminars and speaking engagements. Your feedback, words of encouragement, testimonials, and requests for me to write this book have been my true inspiration.

Most of all, thanks Coach!

Contents

The Shoes of the Fisherman

from the novel by Maurice L. West

"Yesterday I met a whole man. It is a rare experience, but always an illuminating and ennobling one. It costs so much to be a full human being that there are very few who have the enlightenment, or the courage, to pay the price... One has to abandon altogether the search for security, and reach out to the risk of living with both arms. One has to embrace the world like a lover, and yet demand no easy return of love. One has to accept pain as a condition of existence. One has to court doubt and darkness as the cost of knowing. One needs a will stubborn in conflict, but apt always to the total acceptance of every consequence of living and dying."

Introduction

Redefining How We View the Universe and Our Place within It

I feel a great sense of urgency to share my message with you because there is so much work ahead for all of us as HUMANS IN TRAINING. We cannot expect to have peace in the world as long as there is no peace in our community, in our family, and in ourselves. Outer conditions in the world are simply a reflection of the inner state of individuals because most of us do not know how to harness our INNERPOWER. As a result, we deny ourselves the life we are meant to live, a life full of love, happiness, success, and abundance. We must learn to strip away all the layers of fears, doubts, and negative energies from our mind so that we may receive the gifts of life. We have to change ourselves because we have to change this world!

HUMANS IN TRAINING is like an owner's manual for daily life. When do we refer to an owner's manual? When we are in need of insight and information.

It has been said that the beginning of wisdom is when we realize how much we do not know. There is so much about our world and ourselves that we have yet to discover! We are witnessing this through the relentless search for *that* which we think would make us happy. However, most of us make the mistake of thinking that the answer to *that* is a *thing* that lies outside of us—the pain and suffering present in our world reflect this.

But let's leave the past behind with all its pain, failures, and disappointments; it is gone and we cannot do anything about it. Furthermore, when we focus on the past, it does nothing but stunt our growth, and we become stagnant. So let's take action and make life work for us instead of our working for life. Are you ready to embrace life and see it as both a challenge and an opportunity for growth?

This book represents the approach presented in my seminars and workshops and is intended to be an enlightening and encouraging guide to who we are, why we are here, and our place and purpose in the great scheme of things. It is written for both the beginner and the advanced player in what I refer to as the Game of Life. The secret to living this approach as it is intended is presented bit by bit in every chapter.

This is the first of several books in the HUMANS IN TRAINING series. Each book lays the foundation for the next that follows, allowing the reader time to absorb and assimilate the messages it contains. The purpose of HUMANS IN TRAINING—Book One is to make you familiar with the founding principles behind the INNERPOWER approach and THE SCIENCE OF WHOLE-BEING CONDITIONING, an inner science designed to reveal the potential within every human being. With this book, you will gain a deeper understanding of yourself and your purpose. Book two will move on to INNERPOWER and THE SCIENCE OF WHOLE-BEING CONDITIONING *in action*. Here, you will find a series of practical exercises to help you to recondition your whole life, inside and out, so that you may take your life in the direction you desire. You will be encouraged to perform these exercises daily and, if practiced faithfully, you will experience a tremendous change in your life and consciousness. Book three will advance to the INNERLAWS, where you will develop a better understanding of how to achieve harmony on all levels.

Your interpretation of INNERPOWER and THE SCIENCE OF WHOLE-BEING CONDITIONING in book one will be as unique and different as you are. It is my hope that you will take the time to read this book more than once, each time as a new person. As you read, think of each chapter as a pane of glass in a large window. Each chapter read, represents another clear windowpane, until eventually you can see through the entire window.

It is a privilege to share my message with you.

Jay

Reader Beware! This is not a quick-fix book—it has been designed as a tool of self-discovery for those who want to play at the highest level.

Attention:

This book has been written with the awareness that you, the reader, are both a spiritual and a creative being.

In order to excel at any game—hockey, golf, chess—we must become a student of it! We must learn the rules, study the strategies, and determine what is required of us before we can play. When we have a firm grasp of that knowledge, we are ready to play the game to the best of our ability. The game called "life" must be played in the exact same way if we want to extract the most from it.

Before you begin to read this book, you need to realize that the only thing that can stop you from getting to your next level is you; you are both the problem and the solution.

Most people get excited by the idea of seeing their life improve. However, they are less excited and motivated to do what needs to be done to transform this idea into a reality. They have many dreams, but that is all—just dreams! They lack the courage and faith to step into the unknown and allow the Universe to guide them and materialize their dreams. They give themselves many excuses as to why they should remain in their comfort zone, even though they feel trapped and unhappy staying in it. Many know what actions are required for their highest good, but often their fears and lack of courage to surrender prevent them from moving on to the next level. Over time, their lives become full of dead dreams because they are too busy living and fulfilling someone else's dreams, or they are just too afraid to step out of their small, confined, and safe world and embrace what awaits them in the unknown.

Do you want to be one of these people? Do you want life to pass you by while you do nothing but sit, watch, and make wishes from the sidelines? The time has come for us all to take action! The time has come for us all to create and live our life the way it was intended to be lived—with awareness of our spiritual identity—and not by accident, luck, and chance. Are you ready to empty yourself of all the fears and imaginary limitations that you place upon yourself? Are you ready to reach out to life and live fully and joyfully? I believe it is only through abandoning the old and welcoming the new that we will progress in the Game of Life. I believe each of us is the only person who can change our life; we are our own determining factor. So let's change and change quickly!

To get the most from this book, you must commit to two things:

1. You must be open-minded. Be prepared to have your belief system challenged and be willing to lift your sight a little higher and let it extend to a wider horizon.

2. You must be prepared to work on both the inner and outer levels.

As you progress, you will gain insight into how the Game of Life is played and what your life has been preparing you for. Your training will begin from deep within yourself and gradually work its way to the surface to manifest in the outer world for all to see. Trust in the process, and you will prove to yourself that by doing what is required, you will achieve what you really want out of life.

Are you up to the challenge that awaits you? Are you ready to live beyond your imaginary and confining limitations? I challenge you to challenge yourself personally, professionally, and spiritually. Do not wait any longer for other people or the circumstances in your life to change—the time is now! Let INNERPOWER put you on the road to self-realization; however, remember that INNERPOWER only provides you with the tools and shows you how to use them—the rest is up to you!

Enjoy the journey!

Jay D. Allen

"Affirmation of life is the spiritual act by which man ceases to live unreflective and begins to devote himself to his life with reverence in order to raise it to its true value. To affirm life is to deepen, to make more inward, and to exalt the will to live."

—Albert Schweitzer

CHAPTER ONE

InnerPower

The most important accomplishment in life is to improve and change ourselves, to know ourselves, to understand why we are here, and to realize our true purpose in life.

Whole-Being—Well-Being

As spiritual and creative beings, why do the majority of men and women go through life only scratching the surface without experiencing the depth of who they are, living only a physical and reactive way of life? We find the greater majority drifting through life dissatisfied, uncertain, and trying to make sense of it all. There has been an enormous increase in knowledge, in technology, and in control over the physical forces of the outer world. But there has *not* been a corresponding increase in inner control, self-knowledge, and self-discipline. The effects of scientific and technological achievements have added tremendous complexity to our lives, creating a level of stress that we have been ill-prepared to handle. We live in a world where many people have what are called "complexes" because we lack both the *spiritual tools* to deal with our complex lives and the *life skills* to chart our own course.

Consider the overall confusion that characterizes our current times, especially on a spiritual level. I find it interesting that in spite of all the scientific and technological advancements, many people still do not know what life is really about, and many do not even slow down long enough to think about it. "Busyness" has become an epidemic! Most people are so caught up in the external procedures and processes of life that it does not occur to them to entertain questions such as, "Who am I?" and "Why am I alive?" Only when they are thrown into a crisis does their awareness surface momentarily. There is so much chaos in the world today because people do not know what the meaning and purpose of life is. As a result, their ambitions and behavior are guided by values that are not in harmony with truth, and this is destructive to both personal and planetary well-being. If there is any blessing to arise out of September 11th, 2001, it is that not only a nation, but also a world, was awakened to dare to ask such questions!

Realization
Humanity is searching for awareness to some of life's fundamental questions. All of our experiences are designed to bring us to the point where we ask what is the meaning of life?

Question:

How much pain and adversity must we endure on both an individual and global level before we finally surrender to the Law of Life?

Only an Effect of Far Deeper Causes

The variety of personal, social, political, and moral crises our world is facing cannot be solved independently, for they are only an effect of far deeper causes! Technology is not the cause of our problems—unbalanced living is. We do not want to lose or ignore all that we have accomplished, but we must regain all that we have forgotten. Until we develop the inner side of our being, we will not be able to use scientific modern technology with wisdom and compassion. The world will not change unless this situation is turned around. We desperately need an overall lifestyle and spiritual makeover in order to meet these challenges, not with fear, but with a positive sense of faith, strength, and inner direction. Only then will we be able to make the most of the opportunities that these times have to offer.

Question:
Without Love and Compassion, what do we have?

> *Realization*
> The inner science of self-control will prove to be as necessary as the outer conquest of nature.

The values of our modern culture are both unhealthy and unbalanced. The opportunities for seeking outer pleasures and distractions have increased dramatically with technological advancements. The result is that people are feeling overstimulated outwardly, yet starved and empty inwardly. We witness this as people search to escape through alcohol, drugs, food, work, television, sports, games, and entertainment. Do you think it is just a coincidence that low self-esteem is becoming an epidemic in our society? When people direct all their attention and energies outwardly, they have no experience of the magnificent Soul within. Without an awareness and expression of the spiritual side of our being, how can we feel good about ourselves?

> *Realization*
> The secret to bringing harmony into the outer circumstances of our life is to establish an inner harmony with our Soul.

Balancing Spirituality, Science, and Making Things Happen!

The journey you are now beginning is one of self-discovery and self-expression. A journey where you will explore the inner source of willpower, creative initiative, and other essential qualities necessary for a life of harmony and fulfillment. It is a very unique, integrated, and balanced approach to personal and professional development, which, when combined, will strengthen your spiritual development as well. It is an approach I call INNER-POWER, THE SCIENCE OF WHOLE-BEING CONDITIONING. It is unique because it takes human development to a deeper level—one that allows the individual to experience true growth for the long term and provides consistent results. It is based on the systematic reconditioning of our inner processes that we rely on so heavily, yet tend to ignore. Our current unconscious conditioning has molded us into who we are today, and our lives are a reflection of this. INNER-POWER, THE SCIENCE OF WHOLE-BEING CONDITIONING, will help you to identify for yourself that which no longer serves you for your highest good, transforming your life to a *whole* new level.

Before we begin, I want to make it very clear that I cannot teach you anything that you do not already know on some level. Galileo once said, "You cannot teach people anything new, only help them discover the truth they already know and let them live it out."

INNERPOWER teaches you to go within yourself for answers and wisdom. You are not likely to discover outside of yourself what you have failed to find within. Often it can feel as if you are remembering something you have forgotten. Many people *think* they understand, but this is precisely what prevents them from seeing the whole picture.

Question:

Do you know someone who does not know that they do not know, but thinks they do know?

My objective is to give you a means to perceive your life differently—to refine your concept of personal, spiritual, and business success. I want to open your heart to the possibilities of daily life, inspire you to discover your meaning and value, and provoke your thinking in how you see yourself and the world happening around you.

In other words, I want you to think in ways you have not thought before so that you can take your life places you have not been before.

To help you accomplish this, I will be comparing the training and success in athletics to the training and success in business, and, more importantly, to the biggest game of all—the Game of Life!

Although most of us tend to view life as something more serious than a game, I deliberately chose this analogy in order to help you better understand—

- the INNERPOWER approach
- the world we live in
- ourselves
- our purpose.

Humans In Training—a Work in Progress!

Life is like a game in the sense that we are all in training—HUMANS IN TRAINING, players and students of the same game. As with any sport or practice, life demands discipline, focus, and determination in order to succeed. First of all, in order to play our best, we need to learn the rules of the game. Similarly, in the Game of Life, we need to understand the world we live in, for there are *laws of right behavior* built into this world that we must abide by in order to lead a harmonious life with ourselves and our surroundings. Second, in an athletic game, we need to know who our competition is in order to prepare a game plan. In the same way, in the Game of Life, we must know and understand ourselves because we are the only ones who can stop ourselves from "winning." Finally, in sports we need to develop the necessary skills to perform to our potential. In the Game of Life, we need to develop our INNERPOWER and learn essential life skills so we can play at life's highest level and know what it is to win. As we would for any game or profession, in order to excel, you and I must first acknowledge that we are *students* of life, and then we must do our homework!

> ## Realization
> For the student of life, every person and every experience becomes a teacher.

The Object of the Game

Unfortunately, as dynamic and intricate as we are, we came without an owner's manual! Or perhaps more accurately, we have not recognized it or correctly understood it. It is the responsibility of each individual to learn how to play. We are not taught this information in school or at work, so where are we supposed to learn it?

As we arrive at a clear understanding of what it really means to be HUMANS IN TRAINING and understand the object of the game, we can then proceed to consciously work in harmony with the Universe and ourselves. Then, and only then, as we discover our true identity, will we experience our immense spiritual and creative potential and see progress in all areas of our lives.

Exercising Our Mental, Emotional, and Spiritual Muscles

The purpose of this book is to help you develop your inner strength through a system of *inner circuit training*. In order to achieve this, you must begin to exercise beyond the physical—to the mental, the emotional, and, most importantly, the inner Self—to discover the power that lies within you. Any strength, inner or outer, can be developed only through practice and effort, step by step, and must be practiced faithfully, as one would for music or mathematics, until that place of knowing is reached.

Realization
Life is all a matter of training ourselves.

Our competition in the Game of Life is anyone or anything that takes us away from fulfilling our life purpose and experiencing our INNERPOWER. Ultimately, however, we are the only ones who can stop ourselves from advancing to the next level. Nothing and no one outside of ourselves can stop us from fulfilling our life purpose and experiencing our INNERPOWER—unless we assign them the power to do so. We are in control of our game and no one else! Now that we understand that we are our own competition, it is important to study and know the competitor!

Although I make comparisons between the training in athletics and the training in the Game of Life, I want to make it clear to you that this is not a book about sports—it is all about you! The emphasis is on the *training* as it relates to people of all ages or occupations, whether they are a business person, a homemaker, a teacher, or a doctor. My challenge has always been how to express these ideas in a language that the majority of people will understand, relate to, and assimilate. Each of us can relate to the physical; we all have in common a physical body, and we all experience life in a physical world. Fortunately, the same proven training principles that work on the physical level apply to the inner levels as well. While you practice the INNERPOWER approach, I encourage you to personalize it by substituting any word that I may use for one that you can better identify with, one that fits the art, practice, or beliefs in your life. For example, I use the words Spirit, God, Universe, Creator, and Coach interchangeably; you may choose the word that best reflects you.

InnerPower Is Both an approach and a Way of Life

The INNERPOWER approach is simple: *Everything we need, we already have . . . we must simply learn how to use what has already been created within.*

We only need to know that we already have the power within to accomplish anything, and then we need to exercise that power. Everything we are seeking—and I mean everything—already exists deep inside us in its pristine state, waiting to be awakened and used by us. INNERPOWER has to be cultivated; it is already there, but it needs to be brought out. As fire is latent in wood, and flowers lie dormant in seeds, your power begins within. What we are referring to here is a philosophical shift, leading to a shift of consciousness!

INNERPOWER is a way of life. It is not a diet or a quick-fix. It is a way of thinking, feeling, and conducting our life, which, when applied consistently on a daily basis, will allow anyone to experience for themselves the tangible results of improved levels of health, performance, productivity, and overall quality of life, without the inconsistent results and ultimate failure that quick-fix solutions give us. It also means getting back to a natural way of living by establishing a system of beliefs and constructive habits, on all levels, to give us the quality of life that we are all seeking. This is done through harmonizing all of our thoughts, feelings, words, and actions according to Universal Law.

Realization
It is always within our power to put our lives in tune with divine harmony and healing.

"There is one light but many lamps."
—Proverb

Shifting Gears

I compare the way in which many people live their lives to a Formula One race car that is stuck in first gear. It is the finest motor vehicle on the planet, set up perfectly to perform to its fullest potential, but it is as if we had been living our entire life driving this high-powered vehicle stuck in first gear. We know inherently that the car has the potential for greater performance, yet we are not sure how to access it, so we rev the engine higher and higher, until in frustration we begin to blame the vehicle, thinking this is where the problem is. The vehicle is perfect! Unfortunately, we have never learned how to use the clutch, which would allow us to switch gears. Consequently, we do not know what it is like to shift into second, third, and fourth gear and cruise at the higher levels we were designed to operate on. However, through the understanding that consciousness is the clutch, we can begin to gradually experience life in the higher gears and use more of our potential power. When we experience this, we can never imagine going back to a lower gear or to where we were before.

INNERPOWER is the process of expanding our consciousness from first gear to second, from second to third, and so on, to achieve overall success. It is the power within that allows us to shape and create our life exactly as we desire. It also eliminates bad habits or anything that keeps us from experiencing our truest Self and demonstrating our fullest potential. It is the journey that takes human development to a deeper level, one that enables the individual, as well as the team, to experience true growth for the long term.

The founding principle of INNERPOWER is based on the fact that to achieve our full potential personally, professionally, and spiritually, we must first build and operate from a well-constructed *foundation,* the starting point of all success—a foundation based on Wisdom, Love, and Truth.

> ## *Realization*
> The truth is the truth; it always has been and forever will be.

A Checklist for the Journey

A model I like to use that accurately demonstrates what INNERPOWER represents is the following: On any journey we wish to take, we need three essential components—an accurate *map,* an efficient *vehicle,* and a sufficient quantity and quality of *fuel.*

First we begin by using the *right map,* or we risk getting lost. The only thing worse than being lost is not knowing that we are lost; if we were lost and did not know it, how could we ever hope to get back on track? A map provides an accurate *reference point* to compare where we are now to where we want to go, and it shows the most efficient way to get there. With the right map, we can never get lost, assuming of course that we know where we are and where we want to go, and that we have an understanding of the art of map reading.

For example, if I am trying to find my way around one city but I am using the map of another city, it does not matter how hard I work or how motivated I am to get to where I want to go, the map will never do the job. Most of us have experienced how easy it is to drift off course, and some people only make matters worse when they do not like to ask for directions! Therefore, each of us needs to have our own map, but not just any map, it has to be the right map, the one that can lead us to where we want to be, personally, professionally, and spiritually.

Second, if we do not have the *proper vehicle*, or if our vehicle keeps breaking down, we will not be able to complete the trip, or, at best, it will be a very long and difficult journey. If I want this vehicle to work, I'd better learn how to use and care for it.

We do not need to know all the technical details about how an engine works in order to drive the vehicle properly, but we certainly do need to know *how* to drive and understand the *rules* of the road if we are to arrive safely!

Finally, we can have the right map and even the right vehicle, but without the right quantity and quality of *fuel*, we are not going to get very far.

In each of our lives, our *mind* is the *map*, our *body* the *vehicle*, and our *emotions* the *fuel* that drives our spiritual being. Together, they form the core *foundation* of who and what we are. Therefore, the special needs of each must be met.

The Three Circles of Self-Understanding

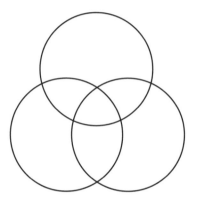

INNERPOWER is the understanding of the interdependent relationships between mind, body, and emotions. These areas are so closely interrelated that you cannot separate one from the other. The model of the three circles clearly illustrates this relationship—one system with three phases. Each circle (or phase) is a self-operative process within the single system. Recognize that there is not a single phase that functions independently of the whole; each phase is but a working out of the single system. This means we can train within each phase independently, yet any change in one area impacts the whole. An imbalance in one area will naturally affect the others, so it is important to work on each. Understanding how the mind, body, and emotions interrelate and act as a hologram can make a big impact on our overall success and quality of life.

INNERPOWER is the *practice* of habitually developing, balancing, and unifying the mental, emotional, and physical qualities until all are one, creating a whole greater than the sum of all its parts. In other words, it is called *Integrated Inner Balance*, whereby our thoughts, feelings, words, and actions are authentic and in harmony not only with each other, but also with our inner Self— our Soul. Our inner Self is our inward sense of what is right, our deepest intuition, as well as our connection with our Creator.

> *Realization*
> InnerPower is more than feeling physically and mentally well. It means that one is whole spiritually, that one feels good, sometimes in spite of what is happening in or around the body.

Becoming a Completed Circle

INNERPOWER is about bringing a *whole* new level of passion, presence, purpose, and commitment to daily living. As we do this, we will experience a different quality of life. INNERPOWER is movement, it is change, it is growth; it calls for you to be completely dedicated to the possibility of experiencing Heaven right here on earth, because without commitment, you will be tempted to give up somewhere along the way. INNER-POWER is not for the person with a weak will or lack of courage. This is beautifully expressed in the excerpt from *The Shoes of the Fisherman* that I quoted for you at the beginning of this book. Unless you are focused and completely dedicated to the development of INNERPOWER in your life, you can easily be thrown off balance by the many strange or negative forces entering your life.

Balancing Inner Needs with Outer Demands

We all recognize the need for balance in our lives. Physical life, for example, depends on a delicate balance of body temperature, blood chemistry, and body weight. Overall balance requires one to achieve not only outer but inner balance as well. Inner balance is a combination of mental, emotional, physical, and spiritual balance. It requires that all our inner functions and outer activities be congruent and in perfect harmony with each other. If all our thoughts, feelings, words, and actions are unified and in harmony, we achieve an inner balance, which eventually leads to the achievement of outer balance. The tricky part is to be aware of when we are out of balance. This can be very subtle because anything we do, we can overdo or underdo. There is no formula for balance; it differs for each individual because we are all unique. Therefore, to live in a state of balance and inner peace, we must continually ask ourselves, "Where might I be out of balance?" and then learn to listen.

The mind, body, emotions, and inner Self are so intimately connected that an imbalance in one will naturally affect the others. When we are out of shape physically, it is very obvious —all we have to do is look in the mirror. However, it is much more difficult to figure out how out of shape we are mentally, emotionally, or spiritually, simply because we have nothing tangible to compare ourselves to. When we are wrong, what is right feels wrong; or when we are out of balance, what is in balance feels out of balance. This is because we measure the world with the yardstick of our learned values, many of which are confined, limited, or unexamined for accuracy. What we are missing is a consistent *reference point*, one that is complete, perfect, and whole—a centered place that we can go to whenever we wish to experience perfect mental, emotional, or spiritual balance. We need this reference point to compare to our current state of inner balance so as to determine to what extent we are in, or out of, balance.

Out with the Old, In with the New

This point was clearly illustrated to me one day while at a driving range hitting golf balls. I thought I was doing great, and when I compared myself with everyone around me, I became even more convinced of my abilities. Just as I was feeling really confident about myself and my swing, a young lady approached me and told me that my grip was wrong! My defense mechanism quickly came to the rescue and I began to *justify* how I was doing just fine, thank you. I gave her many good reasons and told her that, in fact, compared to everyone else, I was hitting the ball farther. She politely and calmly backed away from me and said that she could see that I was doing "just fine," but thought I might want to improve and that was all she had wanted to tell me.

As I stood there already feeling embarrassed, she introduced herself as the club pro! I immediately apologized for my behavior and asked for her help. She proceeded to show me the necessary changes to correct my grip and I quickly explained to her how awkward the changes felt. She said, "Of course they do, when you're wrong, what's right feels wrong!" Just as in life, often when we are out of balance, what is in balance feels out of balance. It took several months for the new and improved grip to feel normal, but I could see a significant difference in my game. Now I not only had greater *control*, but also more shot *opportunities* available to me, and I could never imagine going back to my old grip. Now I had a new reference point to compare my grip to. If the club pro had not demonstrated the correct grip to me, I would have gone on believing that my grip was right. Having a reference point is extremely important if we wish to discover how on or off track we are to building a strong foundation. Is this not what each of us needs in our lives?

> *"The only thing more expensive than a professional is an amateur!"*
> —Anonymous

To experience INNERPOWER, we have to recondition ourselves from the inside out. This means we have to reverse the way we have been living our lives up to this point. INNERPOWER leads to leadership of a different type— Self-Leadership—allowing no one and nothing outside of ourselves to determine and dictate our thoughts, feelings, words, and actions.

Realization
Taking back control begins on the inside at the deepest levels. If we are not in control within, we will never feel in control of our life.

Choose Not to Give Away Your Power

One of my favorite quotes is from Eleanor Roosevelt, who once said, "No one can make you feel inferior without your consent." If you think about it, no one can make you think, feel, say, or do anything without your permission. This applies whether the feelings are positive or negative—no one can make you feel happy or sad without your consent. No one can bring out in us, or make us feel, anything that we ourselves do not have within or that we refuse to express.

Each of us is our final decision maker if we choose to be. However, most people spend all their energy reacting and relating to a never-ending stream of disorganized, random, and reactive thoughts—our own and others'. Is it any wonder we get so overwhelmed and do not feel in control of our lives? Why let your mind get bogged down by little annoyances that you allow to upset you? Do not waste your time and energy. A perfect example is when you are driving a car; do you easily allow other drivers to control your mood? If your mental attitude changes constantly under the pressure of tests and trials, you are losing in the Game of Life.

Realization
The individual who is undefeated within is truly a victorious person.

Question:

What percentage of your expression is deliberately determined by you?

Any power that anyone or anything seems to have over an individual comes from the power that this individual has assigned to that person, thing, or condition. The power is always within us and works according to the direction that we give it!

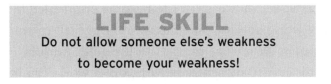

LIFE SKILL
Do not allow someone else's weakness
to become your weakness!

Living in Two Worlds Simultaneously

We completely reverse ourselves when we work from the outside in, or when we work merely for external results that we imagine will satisfy us.

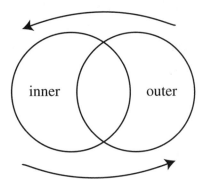

inner   outer

We live in two worlds simultaneously: the inner world of our thoughts, ideas, and emotions, and the outer world of the circumstances and situations that happen to us—our physical reality. We think of these as one, yet they are separate and interdependent. For example, we can be in one place physically, let's say in a car, and be somewhere else mentally and emotionally. Many people arrive at their destination on "cruise control" with little or no memory of how they got there! As we increase our understanding of how these two worlds influence each other, we see how easy it is to become dominated by the outer world and use the inner world only as a mirror for the outer. We are like puppets to the outer world!

It is easy to recognize how the outer world can influence and affect the inner world, which is how most people choose to live. To experience our INNERPOWER, we must reverse this process. When we understand how the inner world influences and affects the outer world, we can recognize that *all of Life* is a process of inward force working itself into outward form! Like the flower that began as a seed or the invention that began as a thought, we develop insight into the creative process that is our life. Once we recognize that any absence of harmony on the external level indicates a corresponding absence of inner harmony, we regain our freedom and power. Now we know where to look!

> ## Realization
> **Everything visible is the result of the invisible.**

Pulling Our Own Strings

We are creative beings, and as such, our tools include our thoughts, feelings, and imagination, which guide our words and actions. We can put these tools to constructive use with the proper guidance of *willpower* and *reason*—again, properties of the inner world—or we can spend our lives reacting to things beyond our control. The choice is ours.

Question:

If our inner consciousness is such a powerful and influential force in our lives, and in fact the main reason for our success, happiness, and quality of life, then why is it the least examined, taught, and understood part of who we are?

Check the Percentages

An important element in what led me to create INNER-POWER was that as an athlete, I had always been told that my performance was at least 80 percent mental. If this was indeed the case, why was it that we would spend 100 percent of our time focused on developing 20 percent of the results? We would spend up to two hours every day exercising our physical skills and techniques, and ignore the other 80 percent—the inner aspects of performance. This did not make any sense to me, and I could never get a satisfactory answer from a coach.

Question:

In business and, more importantly, in the bigger Game of Life, would you agree that success is at least 80 percent mental? And if so, why is the most critical aspect the one that is the most neglected?

Training from the Inside Out

As I began in business, I took as many training courses as I could, only to find most of the teaching to be focused on making only behavioral changes—the 20 percent of physical skills and techniques. Tired of short-term and inconsistent results, I finally came to the conclusion that if we are serious about getting results, we must first become a different person on the inside in order to experience tangible and lasting results on the outside. I realized that all change is, in fact, from the inner to the outer. As we change and raise our consciousness, new ways and new ideas will unfold step by step, and gradually the world will transform with us.

INNERPOWER is the realization that physical skill and technique alone are not enough, especially if the mind is easily distracted or the emotions are in turmoil. I am sure we all know someone who has the talent but is lacking the mental and emotional strength and toughness needed to perform and persevere until the goal is reached.

Question:

Do you know anyone who has more potential than they are currently demonstrating on a consistent and regular basis, where talent or skill is not the problem?

I see that person every time I look in the mirror. We, all HUMANS IN TRAINING, have to continually work on ourselves until we become the ruler of our own kingdom, mastering all the functions, activities, and events going on inside and outside of ourselves. Do you believe it is possible? And what has it cost us in the past for not using our ability to effectively manage and control our mental and emotional states? What price have we paid?

Self-Empowerment 101

I remember speaking to the senior students at a college and receiving a wonderful standing ovation. As soon as I stepped off the stage, many of the students came rushing towards me. I will never forget one young man in particular. He grabbed me by my jacket almost angrily, looked me right in the eye and said, "Why don't they teach us this stuff in school?" I only wish I had had an answer for him. I first read the classic *Think and Grow Rich* by Napoleon Hill when I was eighteen years old. I purchased the book through an infomercial at three o'clock in the morning. After reading this book, I was a little upset and even more confused. Why didn't someone give me this book earlier in my life? Why didn't we study this in school? I could certainly appreciate Shakespeare and his great work, but it was not preparing me for my future or moving me closer to better understanding my potential. Now I was getting a glimpse of the possibilities. I began reading books that would help me achieve my goals and answer those tough questions we all ask ourselves about the meaning and purpose of life. I found there was great wisdom available; however, I remained frustrated that I could not find a practical system to incorporate these teachings into daily life, and there was no education system where I could get a degree in what I really wanted to learn. It was at this time that I decided to begin to create what I desperately wanted to learn.

Wouldn't it be wonderful to expand our educational systems to include INNERPOWER and THE SCIENCE OF WHOLE-BEING CONDITIONING? If we could combine practical tools for developing a strong sense of Self with the appreciation of great literature, science, and the arts, we would get a much more balanced education and, as a result, *experience* the life we are designed to live. I believe our educational system needs to be restructured, for it is now only floating on the surface of life without touching the depths of who we really are.

Understanding versus Realization

It is not what we know *about* something, but rather what we know *of* it that makes the difference. Understanding is one-dimensional—the comprehension of the intellect—and leads to acquired knowledge. Realization, on the other hand, is multi-dimensional. It is the simultaneous comprehension of the whole person—mentally as thoughts, emotionally as feelings, and physically as instincts—and comes only from direct experience. For example, I could describe to you how an orange tastes and you could understand my words; however, it is only when you have experienced it with each of your senses that you truly realize what an orange is. Otherwise I could have been describing a grapefruit and you would never have known it! My objective is for you to not merely *read* about INNERPOWER—I want you to *taste* it!

> ## *Realization*
> ### To know and not to do is not to know!

Often we think we understand; however, real understanding comes only by doing, not just through believing or intellectualizing. Only experience and action have the potential power to turn knowledge into wisdom. We know we understand when our actions change!

Understanding = Knowledge   Realization = Experience

Perhaps this is why so many people understand or think they understand, but they just do not get it! Thinking that they do understand is often what holds people back from getting to the next level. What they understand is where they are at, presently, yet *understanding is infinite.* There is always another level to get to, demanding participation and an open mind. Please recall my earlier message: People struggle not because of what they know but because of what they do not know!

> ## *Realization*
> ### InnerPower is the process of living our life, of believing and actually experiencing.

I have witnessed this many times while teaching my seminar. Towards the end, some participants will reveal to me that they understand what INNERPOWER is all about. This is usually the first sign that they do not! I explain to them that every time I teach the program, I learn something new, and this helps me to realize how much I do not know and how dynamic and intelligent the Universe really is. I tell them that what they understand is only from their own present level of consciousness; however, there is always another level of understanding to get to. Interestingly, often participants who have been through the course more than once share with me that after the first time, they thought they understood; however, after the second experience, they realized how much more they had yet to learn. They were starting to get it! The beginning of wisdom is when you realize how much you do not know.

Realization
The difference between success and failure is a difference in understanding. Even more important is where that understanding leads—to a deeper inner realization of our true identity.

*"Experience is not what happens,
but what we do with what happens."*
—Aldous Huxley

Autobiography in Five Short Chapters

1.

I walk down the street.
There is a deep hole in the sidewalk.
I fall in,
I am lost ... I am helpless.
It isn't my fault.
It takes me forever to find a way out.

2.

I walk down the same street.
There is a deep hole in the sidewalk.
I pretend I don't see it.
I fall in again.
I can't believe I am in the same place.
But it isn't my fault.
It still takes a long time to get out.

3.

I walk down the same street.
There is a deep hole in the sidewalk.
I see it is there.
I still fall in ... it's a habit.
I know where I am.
It is my fault.
I get out immediately.

4.

I walk down the same street.
There is a deep hole in the sidewalk.
I walk around it.

5.

I walk down another street.

Portia Nelson

Mental Power—MIND

The key to your InnerPower is the mind. What an opportunity to develop this marvelous machine whose full capacity has hardly been tapped! Such immense power is in our minds, yet science has not explored its depths. Technologically, we live in a very advanced civilization, yet we remain in ignorance of this amazing instrument of power. We often hear how we use only a small portion of our brainpower. What I find even more amazing is that we have the power to exercise our mind—to control what our mind thinks instead of being controlled by it. If you examine yourself closely—the action of mind over matter, or mind over physical body—you will discover that each individual is a power in themselves.

You are extremely powerful because your mind is extremely powerful. Your mind possesses innumerable powers—more than you can ever imagine—that must be awakened if you want to access them. Through proper training of the mind, we can learn to harness its power so that it can continually move us towards the achievement of our goals and our purpose. I have heard of the mind being compared to a barking dog. We do not have to get rid of the dog; we must simply train it! The longer we wait, the more difficult it gets.

Realization
Thought is a force, the most potent force in the Universe; it has tremendous power but requires the necessary training to bring it forth constructively.

Most people go busily about their daily activities pre-occupied by a continuous stream of disorganized, random, and reactive thoughts. Is it any wonder that most people live their life in a constant state of stress, feeling overwhelmed and not in control? Think of the mind as a television set—we unconsciously give permission to anyone or anything outside of ourselves to change our stations at will. We give away our power by giving away control of the remote!

We are constantly bathed in an energetic pool of thoughts, our own and those of others, which can have a tremendous impact, especially on those of us who are easily influenced by the thoughts of those around them. Until we begin to consciously think for ourselves, our thoughts may not really be our own, but the thoughts of others that enter our mind and make us believe that we are actually thinking those thoughts. This may seem very odd to you, yet it is true. Recognize in your own life how easily your thoughts are influenced by the company you keep!

Children, for example, are highly susceptible to this. They can be so sensitive and receptive to the thoughts of others that they may end up manifesting the fears of those closest to them. Parents may subconsciously attract illness to their child if they constantly fear for their health, always watching for symptoms. Their expectation of illness only prepares the way for it. We do not want to ignore illness or not take preventive measures, but we don't want to create it. If illness does, in fact, arise, we need to mentally focus on improved health and well-being instead of holding on to the idea of illness.

It is time to take back the remote control from others! As we begin to consciously choose what station—or thoughts—we pay attention to, with daily practice, we can eventually control the *volume*. In other words, we exercise clear thinking when we remove the "commercials" of restlessness—all the thoughts unrelated to our desired focus—in the television set of our mind.

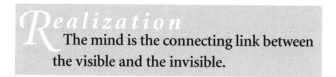

Realization
The mind is the connecting link between the visible and the invisible.

Psychological Antiques

All the great teachers and spiritual masters have warned us to be careful of how and what we think because thought is energy—an actual living thing. We create the world with our thoughts. We are responsible for our thoughts, for we have the power to control not only what we think, but also the kind of thoughts that enter our mind. People of like thoughts are attracted to each other, so no matter where you go, you will attract to yourself, knowingly or unknowingly, what corresponds to your dominant quality of thought. So again, be careful about what you think! Our world is a reflection of our thoughts. Everything exists first on the plane of thought and eventually spirals down to the physical plane. Our thoughts are the most common thing in our life; we take for granted the thousands of thoughts that we think each day. In fact, of the over sixty thousand thoughts we think on a daily basis, up to 95 percent are the same thoughts day after day. Is it any wonder some people and circumstances never seem to change? What was the last deliberate thought you had? How predictable are you?

Realization
As long as your thoughts and behavior are predictable, you are easily manipulated!

To attract new experiences or opportunities into our lives, we must first learn to control our thoughts and develop new habits of thinking. If we persist in thinking a certain way, those thoughts eventually become actions—from thought, all action springs. Just as our thoughts can limit and trap us into a certain state of mind, they also have the power to liberate us from any of our imaginary limitations. To change ourselves, we have to begin with our thoughts.

All that is necessary is to change our thought structure. We need to build a dominant thought structure, one that will allow us to realize more of our potential.

Above or Below an Animal

I find it amazing that an animal is incapable of thinking negatively or developing an adverse thought structure and therefore never loses its instinct or intuition. As

HUMANS IN TRAINING, we can go below the animal level, where we are ruled by random impulses and desires, and engage in selfish and destructive behavior of thought, feeling, word, and action. At this level, we lose touch with our intuition and feel powerless—in other words, we experience *victim consciousness.* We can also rise above the animal level, because we have the power to not only control, but also influence our thought structure by exercising our creativity. Do we consciously exercise this power? At this higher level, our intuition is strong, clear, and powerful, and therefore so are we. Most of us are somewhere in between these two levels.

> *Realization*
> The conquest of the internal nature should be the primary occupation of a human being, otherwise we are no higher than an animal!

Most of us go through our waking hours taking little, if any, notice of our thoughts or of how our mind functions, moves, and operates. For the most part, we misdirect our mental energy, or it dissipates into various channels of useless concerns. We eat, speak, work, think, and play with minimal awareness of what is actually going on in our mind. If you develop the habit of watching your thoughts, you can clearly understand how the mind works and the power it has. You can practice awareness in your daily life by first noticing how the mind randomly bounces between the past and the future, and how little time is given to the present. As you advance further into the practice of awareness, the mysteries of the mind will gradually be revealed to you. Is your mind now working for you or against you? Do your thoughts strengthen you or weaken you? As we draw into our life what we hold in our mind, it is time to empty everything from our mind that no longer serves us for our highest good. Empty it by choosing to focus on the greatest vision you could ever imagine for your life.

Realization
Success is determined by our habitual trend of thought. So which is the stronger in you—success thoughts or failure thoughts?

"The world is what we think it is. If we can change our thoughts, we can change the world."
—H.M. Tomlinson

Emotional Power–HEART

Most of us do not understand the link between our emotions and a healthy, balanced life. Some people have even died of grief over a sudden tragic event or of joy over wonderful news. In such cases, emotion becomes too strong for the body to withstand, and so it collapses and dies. What have we been taught about developing and accepting our emotions? Millions of people worldwide suffer from depression, phobias, fears, anxiety, or stress. This is evidence that as a society, we have not been taught much about the importance of understanding the emotions and their effects. As a result, the majority of us do not know how to use them to attract and cultivate positive emotional energies within ourselves—emotional energies that can cure, heal, or uplift our whole being. Begin to think of e-motion as energy in motion!

Realization
E-motional energy demands release!

It is everyone's responsibility to learn about and understand emotional power and what it can do for or against us. We can learn to experience our feelings fully, instead of suppressing them and then enduring the physical symptoms that occur as a result of not expressing them. When our emotions run wildly, they can be extremely damaging. Many diseases and illnesses are the result of mismanaged emotional energy because we are unaware of the immense power that we are working with. Congestion of emotions such as hatred, criticism, resentment, anger, and jealousy tear down the cells of the body. Even love, when not shared and given freely, becomes a selfish love, which turns back destructively on the individual. INNERPOWER is learning to manage and use our emotions to heal ourselves and others, rather than injecting fears, limitations, or suppression. Cultivating happiness, love, and peace, so as to develop uplifting and healing emotional energies, benefits everyone.

> ## Realization
> Sickness and unhappiness come from violation of the Law of Love.

When the emotions are directed, they are a source of strength for great achievements. Let me give you an example to illustrate the power and use of an emotion. There was a woman, born mute, who woke up one night to find that her house was on fire. The shock of realizing that she might be burned alive made her scream out loud for help, and she woke up everyone in her home. It was the power of her fear that restored the contact between her nervous system and her vocal cords. This is a very rare case, but it has occurred in history. The emotion of fear is to be used *only* for physical survival. When the emotions are used correctly, they are extremely powerful and can even heal a physical condition that is considered incurable by modern medical science. However, many people have fears even when their life is not in danger. Most of their fears are imaginary, and in the most extreme cases, their fears can cause them to become ill and can paralyze their ability to function.

Another example I came across is that of an employee of a refrigeration company, who was accidentally locked in a freight train's ice chamber with a temperature of forty degrees below zero. Unfortunately, no one heard his shouts for help. He was absolutely terrified and left a record of his suffering scribbled on the walls of the chamber. By the time the train arrived at its destination, he had died. Incredibly, his death was not the result of exposure to sub-zero temperatures, but it was brought about by absolute fear, because on that day, the refrigeration had not been switched on at all!

> *Realization*
> Through the power of emotions, men and women have overcome their limitations and attained a higher purpose in life.

Emotional freedom is a major factor when it comes to effective communication. It is our ability to express ourselves freely, as well as to not feel vulnerable to the ideas and opinions of others. Emotional freedom can be defined as the ability to become centered and even-minded, independent of what may be happening around us—independent of all the turmoil of daily life.

Refuse to get caught up in the life and drama of others. I do not mean for you to ignore the problems and suffering of those around you, rather that you not let them pull you down. If you let yourself be affected in this way, you can become as depressed, helpless, or frustrated as your suffering teammates. Consequently, you are of no use to them and are not able to help them. We must feel compassion and respect for others' journeys, yet detach ourselves in our dealings with them in order to raise them up to a higher level. We need to spend more time working on and improving our own inner life, finding solutions for our teammates, and being a solution ourselves. There is a lot of real inner work that awaits all HUMANS IN TRAINING.

LIFE SKILL
Letting go of compulsive and reactive baggage!

"Imagination is more important than knowledge. Knowledge is limited. Imagination encircles the world."
—Albert Einstein

Physical Power—STRENGTH

Physical life on earth begins and ends with the physical body; respect it. It is a spiritually perfect body once we understand how to use it. Of all the things that science has accomplished, nothing compares to the wonder of the intricately organized human body.

INNERPOWER is the understanding of how the body is linked to both the mind and the emotions so that we may further appreciate and respect the importance of our physical health for living a balanced life. We cannot fool our body. It provides accurate and direct feedback of our mental, emotional, and spiritual well-being, and plays a major role in determining the quality of our life experience. We must learn to listen to and appreciate this vehicle because most physical illnesses have their root cause in the inner levels. If we treat only the body and ignore the root cause, the physical symptoms will reappear sooner or later—if not the same symptoms, then new ones. For any long-lasting healing to take place, we must learn to communicate with our body so that we may look deeper into our whole being.

Realization
Physical disease is caused by a mind, heart, and Soul not at ease.

I am always amazed at how so many people treat their car better than their own body. You would not put mud in your car and expect it to work. Yet this is exactly what many of us do with our physical body. We feed our body with the mud of artificial fertilizers, pesticides, and preservatives; eat excessively; fill ourselves with negative thoughts and emotions; and ignore the inner Self; then we wonder why something goes wrong with our physical health! To achieve a strong, healthy, and sensitive physical body, we need to fully appreciate this vehicle. We can do this with the proper maintenance of natural food, fresh air, exercise, and, of course, meditation.

Our body is the greatest miracle ever in creation—the greatest temple ever built. What are temples built for? Communion with God. We should make use of the body for the purpose for which it was created. It is also the greatest vehicle ever made in the Universe for the purpose of learning, growing, and evolving the consciousness.

> ## Realization
> The human body is an invaluable gift because it serves as the foundation for spiritual realization!

"We become what we repeatedly do.
Excellence then, is not a single act but a habit."
—Aristotle

Inner Self—SOUL

It is the spiritual dimension of life that is the most universal and unifying dimension of all. The spiritual plane is where we find common ground because it is here that we identify and address the needs and aspirations shared by every human being. Modern science will ultimately confirm what has been taught by the spiritual masters for thousands of years about the nature of the Universe. Knowledge obtained through outward means can never fully satisfy the nature of humankind.

Realization
All power to satisfy the Soul lies within.

The failure of outer things to satisfy leads the Soul to seek the power within—this inner place of peace and calm. When we learn to live from the Soul—the inner Self—and not from the mind, everything in life is clear and understandable: We know what we should do, where we should go, and life becomes simple and harmonious. It means that we will be led and instructed from within, and our thoughts will be the outcome of properly exploring the inner Self. That is life as it is intended, life as it is, and life as we must ultimately live it.

We are not adequately nourishing the needs and qualities of the Soul. What is needed is a connection with God, one that flows from both heart and Soul. When we make the effort to change ourselves spiritually, we are helping not only ourselves, but also our family, everyone we come into contact with, our country, and the whole world. Progress must be expanded along spiritual lines if we are to experience our INNERPOWER. Strengthen your faith and determination—what an opportunity to develop this marvelous creation!

> *Realization*
> Within each of us is an inner core of peace that we can learn to access at will.

The Force Is within You

Our true purpose is revealed in the privilege and opportunity of expressing our INNERPOWER. You need only know that you already possess the power within to do anything, then you just have to learn how to *exercise* this power and use it for its intended purpose!

> *Realization*
> It is the vital action of the force of nature that makes a seed grow, for no seed has power within itself; it does not try to grow, it is a container, vehicle, and expression of this force. We are a container, vehicle, and expression of this life force as well!

Charles P. Steinmetz
(1865–1923)

Charles P. Steinmetz, the great electrical engineer, was once asked, "What line of research will see the greatest development during the next fifty years?" He replied, "I think the greatest discovery will be made along spiritual lines. Here is a force which history clearly teaches has been the greatest power in the development of men. Yet we have merely been playing with it and have never seriously studied it as we have the physical forces. Someday people will learn that material things do not bring happiness and are of little use in making men and women creative and powerful. Then the scientists of the world will turn their laboratories over to the study of God and prayer and the spiritual forces, which as yet have hardly been scratched. When this day comes, the world will see more advancement in one generation than it has seen in the past four."

InnerPower

- For the student of life, every person and every experience becomes a teacher.
- Life is all a matter of training ourselves.
- The truth is the truth; it always has been and forever will be.
- You cannot keep a balance unless you have a center.
- Everything visible is the result of the invisible.
- To know and not to do is not to know!
- Thought is a force, the most potent force in the Universe.
- Physical disease is caused by a mind, heart, and Soul not at ease.
- All power to satisfy the Soul lies within.
- Within each of us is an inner core of peace that we can learn to access at will.

*"Once in a while it really strikes
people that they don't have to live in the
way they have been told to."*
—Alan Keightly

CHAPTER TWO

The Science of Whole-Being Conditioning

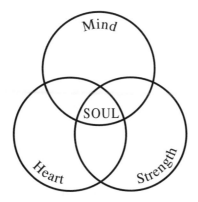

It is the synchronizing of the three circles of life—Mind, Heart, and Strength—*that allows us to experience the power of our* Whole-Being *and gets us to the* Soul *of the matter!*

Self-Transformation through Whole-Being Awareness

THE SCIENCE OF WHOLE-BEING CONDITIONING is the science of gaining control of our inner consciousness, using our mental, emotional, physical, and spiritual powers to create our reality and to achieve all-around success. This is a training method that both explores and demonstrates the intimate relationship between these areas, and shows how, if just one is not fully developed or out of balance, our whole being is out of balance as well.

As I look back and reflect on my experience as an athlete, I recognize many important lessons and principles that apply equally to daily life, for example:

- Success is in direct proportion to *preparation* and *conditioning*.
- Failure and mistakes are a natural and important part of the learning, growth, and development processes.
- There is no success without failures and mistakes.

The more we begin to understand this, the more we develop greater respect for both the *training* and the *training process*. It is essential to recognize that each of us has absolute control over our preparation and conditioning; we simply must make the effort. How powerful this can be!

Who and where we are today, in every aspect of our lives—mentally, emotionally, physically, personally, professionally, and spiritually—is the result of our past preparation and conditioning, or lack of it. We might make a lucky shot or win a play by luck or chance, but the team or the individual that is better prepared and conditioned on all levels is going to be the winner.

So, what does this have to do with you?

"Pay less attention to what others say,
just watch what they do."

—Andrew Carnegie

The Foundation

What do athletes and all successful men and women spend their time on? *The basics*—building a strong foundation to serve as a reliable reference point. When there is a problem or an error, we go back to the foundation to correct it; but what would we do if no foundation had been built? We would keep making the same mistakes over and over, completely unaware of the cause, yet fully aware of the effects. Consequently, we would be unable to correct the mistakes unless or until we were fortunate enough to have someone point out to us where we had gone astray. Sometimes we would win and sometimes we would lose; sometimes we would get it and sometimes we would not, never quite sure why. Sometimes we would have good days, sometimes bad ones; sometimes we would make the sale and sometimes we would not. Sounds frustrating and familiar, doesn't it? Like not being in control? A weak foundation is what causes a person to feel as though everything in life happens randomly without any good reason or higher purpose.

How was your current inner foundation built? It is the responsibility of all HUMANS IN TRAINING to make sure that their foundation is strong. We have to continually and consciously work on building and improving this foundation in order to manage our daily lives effectively. Most people have not even started to understand how weak their foundation is, and that is why they experience life as just a series of random events that are happening without any known cause.

Now consider that a building can be built only as high as the foundation is strong. If we are to take our life to new and higher levels, where do we need to begin working?

> *R**ealization***
> The *Height* of our success is in direct proportion to the *Strength* of our Foundation.

At a construction site, you can always estimate how high a building is going to be by looking at the size and strength of the foundation that is needed to support it. Lack of a strong foundation compromises the entire structure. Similarly in life, we compromise the entire structure of our whole being when we lack a strong inner foundation; that is, when our foundation is based on anything other than universal laws or principles. Just as a chain breaks at its weakest link, we too, will break down physically, mentally, emotionally, or spiritually at our weakest link—the place in the chain or structure of our foundation that is weak.

For greater consistency in life, we must be centered and balanced because only then can we be productive with our time or skill. So, what have we been taught about how to construct an inner foundation for our life—a life built on mental, emotional, and spiritual strength and power? Any type of foundation does not just happen or build itself! It requires constant work and effort. Once the foundation is assured, everything falls into place and progresses as it should. Have you ever noticed how quickly the building goes up once the foundation is properly in place?

Question:

If we want to take our life to the next level, where do we need to begin working?

Start Building!

So, how do you build a strong inner foundation?

In sports, the 20 percent of preparation and conditioning we worked on followed certain training principles: the training was *specific, systematic, progressive,* and *daily*. Recognize that these principles apply equally to any training or skill development.

> *Realization*
> A seed can grow only when it is firmly fixed in the ground.

SPECIFIC

Think about this: When you go to the gym to exercise and your training is random, what type of results do you get? Random results! If your training is specific, you are in control, and you get specific results. If your training is not specific, any means adopted to achieve a goal will essentially fall flat like a huge structure built on a weak foundation.

An important side effect of specific preparation and conditioning is that we feel more *confident,* and our *expectations* change from hoping for a good result to expecting to win and succeed! Recognize that our chances to succeed, as well as our confidence and expectations, are in direct proportion to the amount of specific training and preparation we do, especially over the long term.

With physical training, we can customize the sets and repetitions to get the exact results we desire. Just as we can reshape and recondition ourselves on the physical level, we can do the same on each of the other levels. INNERPOWER is a deliberate reconditioning of these inner qualities.

Question:

We live in a society where most people are physically lazy and out of shape. What kind of shape are we in, mentally, emotionally, and spiritually?

When we are out of shape physically, it is easy to see by looking in the mirror. It is not so easy to recognize when we are out of shape mentally, emotionally, and spiritually, especially without any previous training to serve as an accurate reference point or the skill to tune in to the many signs happening around us. Many people are accustomed to blaming others instead of getting into the spirit of exercising within.

As HUMANS IN TRAINING, we must recognize that the development of the physical body is very specialized, whereas the development of our inner qualities has an impact on every aspect of our life—personal, professional, and spiritual. A strong inner foundation results not only in an improvement in each of these areas, but also in a much greater sense of Self and clarity of purpose.

SYSTEMATIC

Consider the importance of a well-designed Game Plan.

Every one of us can appreciate the ease and efficiency of a well-designed system. Without a system, the result is a flurry of activity with very little or no achievement. It is the responsibility of both the individual players, as well as the team as a whole, to not only learn the system, but also to discipline themselves and persevere until the desired results are achieved.

In athletics, each practice is carefully planned and executed; everything has a purpose. Players work both independently on their skills and *interdependently* as a team, following a carefully planned system. The degree to which each player follows the system determines the overall success of the team.

As Humans In Training, we can learn so much from this! Working on our own individually, as well as helping one another as a team, we can best achieve our true purpose in life. We can help each other to understand that our greatest contribution to world peace is to learn to live in peace within ourselves.

A man I respect and admire is the legendary basketball coach John Wooden. In his coaching days, he would spend up to two hours planning a one-hour practice, and he would keep detailed notes. Imagine if we did this for our life! Imagine if we could learn to spend just one hour every day planning and reviewing our Game of Life, asking ourselves questions such as: Where must I change to improve my inner life? Am I being true to myself and my purpose? What is my purpose? What can I do to bring more love and happiness not only to my life, but also to those around me? Just as coach Wooden didn't leave the outcome of the game to luck or chance, we, too, must learn to do the same with our life. Coach Wooden guided his teams to a record ten NCAA (National Collegiate Athletic Association) basketball championships. To put that in perspective, no other coach has ever won more than three championships!

InnerPower proves the importance of a game plan for life—a Life Plan!

PROGRESSIVE

A step-by-step approach can assure success. Progressively is how we naturally learn—it is the way we learned to walk, talk, read, and write. Failure is also a natural and important part of the learning, growth, and development processes. Progress comes steadily if we prepare ourselves for it—by first learning to crawl, then walk, and finally run. Change works best when we realize that it does not all have to happen at once. Evolution is the natural process of progress, the result of many small, minor changes forward. Every goal can be broken down into small, doable steps, so that the seemingly impossible becomes possible.

Each time we stretch ourselves beyond our comfort zone, we can never return to who we were before. This results in lasting change, which we all want. Each step lays the foundation for the development of the step to follow.

You will discover how important it is not to skip steps; they are all part of the preparation and creative processes. Take little steps before you try to take giant steps!

Rather than making a sudden or dramatic change, we are better off scaling the mountain of success one step at a time. The highest mountain is climbed in the same way as the lowest, by placing one foot in front of the other, one step at a time.

If, while climbing, we are always looking to the top as a measure of our success, it can make for a very long and discouraging journey, especially when the end is nowhere in sight or within reach. Whatever mountain we are climbing in life, if we regard each step of the way as a success, the journey becomes a lot more enjoyable. It also keeps us on track and motivated along the way. Sometimes life can feel like a very high mountain to climb!

*"I learned to speak as one learns to
skate or cycle—by doggedly making a fool
of myself until I got used to it."*
—George Bernard Shaw

DAILY

Life is a daily discipline.

I cannot emphasize strongly enough the importance of daily practice. Repetition! Repetition! Repetition! This is how we all learn. How often do professional athletes practice? Once a week? Once a month? Whenever they feel like it, or whenever they are in the mood? Daily practice is essential if we are to play at the top of our game, whatever that game may be—golf, music, health, or our spiritual life.

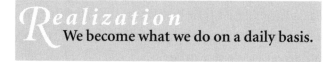

Realization
We become what we do on a daily basis.

We must have a plan, and work that plan daily! Compare the results of training once a week versus training daily. In any endeavor, the results over time are as different as night and day. If we are not consistent in our practice, our consciousness never recognizes a new demand; it changes little and is unable to provide support. Whether physical exercise or meditation practice, the results of training once a day for a short time far outweigh the results of training on and off for a longer period of time.

Greater Consistency

What do all professional golfers have in common? The answer is a "pre-shot" routine. Each golfer has an individual routine that they go through before taking every shot, whether on the practice range or on the course. This provides greater consistency and results. Would you like greater consistency in your life? How about a pre-shot routine for daily life? Why are professional athletes so specific and almost fanatical about their pre-game routines? We know we should not exercise without warming up before and cooling down afterwards because we risk getting injured, but how about life? How about preparing for each day and conditioning on all levels—a mental, emotional, and spiritual warm-up? We hurt only ourselves when we neglect or ignore performing the warm-up and cool-down exercises, which are essential to the development and refinement of our whole being.

We all need to develop a daily routine of training for mental, emotional, physical, and spiritual fitness—a routine that is appropriately suited to the needs, conditions, and environment of each individual.

A Process of Reconditioning

We build our lives around routines and habits, and we can get locked into patterns, even when they do not work. Ask yourself this question: Have your current habits and routines been consciously chosen by you, or are they the result of random conditioning or programming developed over the years? As you become a better student and observe yourself carefully, you will notice that most of what you think, feel, say, and do remains more or less the same. Even if there is an area in your life that you wish to change, your old habits will keep you from moving on unless you strongly determine to no longer be their slave. The good news is that a good habit is as easy to acquire and as difficult to break as a bad one.

Question:

Is what you are doing on a daily basis getting you closer to the things you want to achieve? Is it helping you to become the person you want to be?

I will never forget the conversation I had with a professional coach who shared with me that he felt his team's performance was at least 85 percent mental. He went on to tell me that he did not neglect this critical area by having a sports psychologist speak to his team once a month for forty minutes. Just to make sure that I was hearing him correctly, I confirmed that he spent forty minutes once a month developing 85 percent of the results, and spent up to two hours every day working with the players developing the other 15 percent. He had four assistant coaches to help prepare and teach his system and game plan, but he had no system or game plan with the sports psychologist. Do you see a problem and the inconsistency?

How Is Your Game?

How does this apply to you? We spend so much time preparing and training for a game or an event, and yet what do most people do to prepare and get into condition for their future? Does this make sense? My point is, what type of specific, systematic, and progressive preparation and conditioning are you doing in your life right now on a daily basis to assure your success, happiness, and quality of life? Or are you like most people, just living life, working hard, and hoping for the best?

Try to imagine some of the greatest coaches of all time, such as Vince Lombardi, John Wooden, or Scotty Bowman—all masters of preparation—saying to their players, "Okay guys, we're not prepared or in shape, we don't have a system to follow or a game plan, and we don't know the rules or anything about our competition, so what I want you to do is go out there and work really hard and give it everything you have. We'll just hope for the best and see what happens!" How long do you think they would have a job?

As ridiculous as it may sound, is this not exactly how most people choose to live their lives? They have no definite plan, goal, or purpose, and so they are subject to the winds of change, blown here or there by the circumstances and situations that enter their lives. They wander about life with no aim and are constantly chasing after this or that for a little love, a little happiness, or a little gratification. No wonder they think life is a struggle and they cannot seem to get ahead. We do not leave a simple game to luck or chance, so why our lives?

Preparation begins on the inside at the deepest levels. If we are not in control mentally and emotionally, we will be unable to utilize our physical skills and talents or experience our full potential as HUMANS IN TRAINING.

Realization

If preparation and conditioning are not fully conscious, specific, systematic, progressive, and practiced daily, they are random and so are the results! To see desired results, we must make new demands on ourselves by exercising and learning to recondition our whole being.

Tiger Woods has several personal coaches. How about you? If your first thought is, "Well, he can afford it," the truth is you cannot afford not to! Yet, there is a saying, "When the student is ready, the teacher will appear." The Universe is constantly guiding and sending you exactly what you need to progress in your life, but you need to learn to be open and recognize when help is being sent to you, so that you do not inadvertently reject or push it away. For example, recognize that the Universe has placed this book into your hands and that it is no accident that you are now reading it. Within this book you will undoubtedly find one or more messages that can help to usher you on to the next level, or liberate you from an attachment to a certain attitude, belief, person, or anything that may have paralyzed you for the last seconds, years, or decades. However, you must be open in order to recognize what that message for you is because it is different for everyone. Then you must act on the message as if your life depended on it, because it does!

Question:

How does the mind affect our performance in daily life, and how can we affect the performance of the mind through specific, systematic, and daily training?

The Spiritual Discipline of Integration

I developed THE SCIENCE OF WHOLE-BEING CONDITIONING based on the idea of taking the proven training principle of the 15 percent—the physical level we are currently working on—and applying them to the other 85 percent to get 100 percent of our being working in harmony. As we achieve this level of *wholeness* between the mind, body, and emotions, we will be ready for the next level—our inner Self.

Question:

Do you see yourself as a physical being with a spirit, or as a spiritual being with a body? Where do we need to begin training?

As a society, we seem to accept the idea that we are spiritual and creative beings, yet we remain focused on the physical and material and live mostly reactive lives. Then we wonder why something is missing. Inner work and exploration are essential in controlling the energies of life and consciousness. Until we begin to work on a *causal or spiritual level,* we are attempting to change an effect without first understanding or changing the cause. As long as we mistakingly treat symptoms as the cause, the effects will continue to resurface until we begin the process of healing ourselves. This is a science of living that is universal, timeless, and that you can prove by experimenting on yourself!

In order for this training to be considered a science, it must meet three criteria:

1. It must be *understandable*, and we must be able to *experience* it. It must be possible for us to translate the information, understanding, and awareness into a change of action. You do not have to take my, or anyone else's word for it, simply trust and learn from your own experience. If you exercise physically every day for thirty minutes, you will soon begin to see results, regardless of whether you are skeptical or not. Similarly, if you exercise the mind, emotions, and spirit according to the same training principles, you will soon begin to see the desired results.

2. It must be in accordance with *natural laws* and principles. It involves discovering an already existing and functioning law in the Universe, and then learning to benefit from it in our daily life. Each of us must learn to live in harmony with natural laws on all levels, seen and unseen, known and yet to be discovered. The HUMANS IN TRAINING course is based on the INNERLAWS, which are in accordance with natural laws and principles.

3. It must have *practical application*. If there were no practical application, then no matter how sublime the science, it would be of no value to humankind. Specific tools and techniques help to prepare and integrate the SCIENCE OF WHOLE-BEING CONDITIONING and the INNERLAWS into daily life.

Learning Formula

I created this formula while teaching seminars, in order to clearly illustrate the components necessary to properly learn any subject—to "get it."

Awareness (What) + Understanding (Why) + Action (How) = Realization

Awareness = Observation

We develop awareness by listening carefully to ourselves and to others—becoming conscious of what was previously unconscious—with an even, nonjudgmental mind. Being aware enables us to see clearly the areas of our lives we need to work on. We cannot fix anything until we recognize that it is broken, we cannot regain control until we realize that we have lost control. In the same way, we cannot strengthen our weak links and consistently improve until we become aware of our weaknesses. Expanding our consciousness through self-observation of who we are and how we function as HUMANS IN TRAINING is first a matter of self-awareness. The more we become aware, the more our consciousness expands, giving us more power to further enhance our awareness.

Realization
Awareness of a weakness is the beginning of strength.

Understanding = Knowledge

Understanding is increasing our knowledge of the laws and principles that govern our life and learning the rules of the game and how the Universe is set up for us—equitably and impartially. From my experience, I believe the number-one reason someone does not "get it" is because they do not understand the "why"—why things happen and why we are here, the process of life unfolding. We also need to understand why we need to develop certain relationships in our lives.

> *Realization*
> Understanding is the greatest possession of each Soul.

Action = Tools

Action is putting knowledge into practice by applying the principles and exercises to get results—translating awareness and understanding into a change of action! It is responding to the question, How can I tell what I know until I see what I do? When action is undertaken as defined here, it has the potential to turn knowledge into wisdom. The value of wisdom is not merely in helping us to live life fully and with a purpose, but ultimately in helping us to fulfill our true destiny.

> ## *Realization*
> Action is more powerful than mental and emotional subjectivity.

Only when we combine each of these ingredients successfully, do we give ourselves the necessary foundation to create lasting change, and to experience true Self-Realization.

> ## *Realization*
> Little distinctions can make a huge difference.

We Are the Source of Our Own Turmoil

In the final analysis, only we can control ourselves. We are often discouraged by our inability to do this. What prevents us? The inner doubts, fears, impulses, and unconscious desires and motivations all create an imbalance that leads to mental and physical suffering. When we feel out of control or out of harmony, it is usually because there is a conflict between what we think and what we feel. Our feelings may scream one thing, while our mind demands something else. As long as we have not glimpsed our true identity, we are enslaved to the unexamined habit patterns of our mind. We rarely understand that freedom lies beyond the well-worn grooves of the brain.

The time has come to take a sharp and critical look at how and what we are thinking and feeling, and what we are doing with our life.

If you reflect carefully, you will see that, in reality, your individual freedom is lost because you are an absolute slave to a number of worthless habits. However, when INNERPOWER becomes our habitual way of living, we achieve the results we want on a consistent basis, and life becomes much more enjoyable.

To discover what your habits are, first become aware of how you move into habitual responses when dealing with others—spouse, children, coworkers, boss. Look for patterns in yourself and others. How predictable are you? Recognize that the predictable individual is the easiest to manipulate—ask any kid! As a student of INNER-POWER, you must discover and eliminate all negative or self-defeating habits by constructing new and more effective habits. INNERPOWER habits are servants who will serve you well.

Realization
It is awareness that allows the ordinary to become extraordinary!

Habits Run Our Lives

How does something become a habit? Habits are simply thoughts grooved deeply into the brain. The needle of the mind plays those same tracks over and over because it believes it cannot get rid of a particular thought. Once you perform an action, it leaves an effect or impression on the consciousness. As a result, you are likely to repeat that action. After several repetitions, that inclination is so strengthened that the action becomes a habit. For some people, once is enough! Imagine your habits or actions as if they were clay. Your thoughts mold or shape your habits. Through repetition of your thoughts and actions, you develop mental convictions, or the fire that hardens them into habit patterns. Not only are your thoughts and habits (mind and body) molded into patterns, but your whole life is, too.

Realization
In the hands of an inspired artist, a worthless lump of clay becomes a work of art.

We often hear that it takes twenty-one to thirty days to create a new habit. I believe it takes twenty-one to thirty days of daily practice to gain the support of the subconscious mind, and four to six months to establish a new habit. It is amazing how the same mind that tries to talk us out of doing something new during the first few weeks of practice suddenly begins reminding us to do it. This is further evidence that everything we need, we already have; we must simply learn how to use what has already been created within. A great place to begin is to take time every day to review your HUMANS IN TRAINING Journal, which we will discuss later, as part of your warm-up and cool-down exercises. It takes a strong will to establish this habit, yet once the routine is in place, we realize the power and impact it has on our life. When we occasionally slip off our routine, it feels as though something is missing, urging us to get back on track. Remember that the purpose of the routine is both preparation and conditioning for the game of your life, which is where the action takes place!

> ## Realization
> InnerPower is the most effective force we can use to break free of limiting weaknesses and habits and move into an all-embracing expansion of consciousness.

The Art of Spiritual Living

As long as we are consistent in our ability to communicate what we want, our desire will manifest accordingly. This works in both the positive and negative senses, depending on the nature of the desire. It is to our advantage if we develop the habit of thinking great thoughts and living congruently. We must do the INNERPOWER exercises until it is hard not to do them!

We are unconscious of many habits that control our lives, such as brushing our teeth, combing our hair, tying our shoes, and even driving a car. Have you ever arrived somewhere and found it hard to recall how you got there? It is like living on cruise control, doing almost everything with minimal awareness, unconsciously going through the motions. Is this how you are meant to live?

> ## Realization
> We usually do, not what we wish to do, but only what we are accustomed to doing.

Remember that these habits, peculiar to your nature, are nothing but manifestations of your own thoughts. Your character was molded by none other than yourself. Certainly there are outside influences, but inner acceptance is the determining factor. As long as we remain unaware of our spiritual identity, we remain caught in habits and patterns of the personality, and we cannot experience our INNERPOWER. Our habits control us; we bounce whenever and wherever our habits bounce, so that almost always we are reacting to the world with little capacity to deliberately choose our own actions.

> ## Realization
> It is only when we free ourselves from our bad habits that we are truly free agents. We all have this power!

Take a Moment for Self-Reflection

- What is your habitual trend of thought?
- Do you have the habit of expecting the best out of every situation or the worst?
- When a problem arises, do you have the habit of thinking of it as an obstacle, or do you see it as an opportunity?
- Do you have the habit of supporting your friends, or do you have the habit of criticizing others—not just when you're with them, but when they're not there?
- Do you have the habit of condemning other people, or giving them the benefit of the doubt?
- Do you have the habit of preparing and conditioning yourself on all levels to achieve the life you want?
- What do you habitually tell yourself about yourself?
- Do you have the habit of giving 100 percent effort to everything you do?
- Do you have the habit of making other people's days?
- Do you have the habit of putting disappointment behind you, or do you hang on to it and use it as an excuse?
- Have you developed the habit of being happy and creating success?

The Daffodil Principle

My daughter had telephoned several times to ask me to come to her place in the mountains to see the daffodils before they were over. I wanted to go, but it was a two-hour drive, and I honestly did not have a free day until the following week, but I promised to go the following Tuesday.

That day was cold and rainy but I had promised, so I set out. The tops of the mountains were sheathed in clouds, and after only a few miles up the mountain highway, the road was completely covered with a wet, gray blanket of fog. I slowed to a crawl, my heart pounding as I drove up the hazardous, narrow, and winding road. When I finally walked into Carolyn's house and hugged my grandchildren, I said, "Forget the daffodils, I won't drive another inch!" My daughter smiled calmly and said she was hoping I'd take her to the garage to pick up her car. She assured me it wasn't far, so we bundled up the children and went out to my car.

In a few minutes, with Carolyn at the wheel, I was aware that we were back on the mountain road. "Where are we going?" I exclaimed, distressed to be back on the road in the fog. This wasn't the way to the garage, but Carolyn said we were going the long way—by way of the daffodils. I protested, but Carolyn, with a knowing grin, assured me that it was all right. She said I couldn't miss this experience.

So, like it or not, I was on the way to see some ridiculous daffodils, driving through the thick, gray silence of the mist-wrapped mountaintop at what I thought was risk to life and limb. Soon, we turned onto a small gravel road that branched down into an oak-filled hollow on the side of the mountain.

We parked and walked towards some towering evergreens. There, we saw an inconspicuous, hand-lettered sign: "Daffodil Garden."

We each took a child's hand, and Carolyn led us down a pine needle-covered path that wound through the trees. Oak trees, mountain laurel, shrubs, and bushes clustered on the mountain slope; the green foliage looked dark and monochromatic. I shivered in the damp cold. Then we rounded a corner in the path, and I gasped.

Before me lay the most glorious sight, unexpected and completely splendid. It looked as though someone had taken a great vat of gold and poured it down over the mountain peak and slopes, where it had run into every crevice and over every rise. Even in the mist-filled air, the mountainside was radiant, clothed in massive drifts and waterfalls of daffodils. The flowers were planted in majestic, swirling patterns, great ribbons in every shade of yellow.

It did not matter that the sun was not shining. The brilliance of the daffodils was like the glow of the brightest sunlit day. "But who has done this?" I asked Carolyn, "and how, and why, and when?" I was overflowing with gratitude towards her for having brought me there. This was a once-in-a-lifetime experience.

"It's just one woman," Carolyn answered. "She lives on the property. That's her home." Carolyn pointed to a well-kept, modest little house. We walked up to it, my mind buzzing with questions. On the patio, there was a poster with the heading: "Answers to the Questions I Know You Are Asking."

The first answer was a simple one. "Five thousand bulbs."

The second answer: "One at a time, by one woman, two hands, and two feet."

The third answer: "Began in 1958."

There it was. The Daffodil Principle. For me, that moment was a life-changing experience. I thought of this woman, who, more than thirty-five years before, had begun one bulb at a time to bring her vision of beauty and joy to an obscure mountaintop. One bulb at a time. There was no other way to do it. No short cuts, simply loving the slow process of planting. Loving an achievement that grew so slowly and that bloomed for only three weeks of each year. Just planting one bulb at a time, year after year, had changed the world.

The principle her daffodil garden taught is one of the greatest lessons we can learn. If we move towards our goals and desires one step at a time, often just one baby step at a time, and learn to love the doing, with just a little effort every day, in time we, too, can accomplish magnificent things. We can change the world.

I was suddenly overwhelmed with the implications of what I had seen. "It makes me sad in a way," I admitted to Carolyn. "What might I have accomplished if I had thought of a wonderful goal thirty-five years ago and had worked away at it 'one bulb at a time' through all those years? Just think what I might have been able to achieve!"

My wise daughter summed up the message of the day in her direct way. "Start tomorrow," she said with the same knowing smiles she had worn for most of the morning. Oh, profound wisdom!   *~Jaroldeen Asplund Edwards~*

The Science of Whole-Being Conditioning

- The *Height* of our success is in direct proportion to the *Strength* of our Foundation.
- We become what we do on a daily basis.
- The Mind, Heart, Body, and Spirit are a working team and must be kept in optimal condition!
- The Game of Life can be played successfully only through spiritual understanding.
- Awareness of a weakness is the beginning of strength.
- Understanding is the greatest possession of each Soul.
- Action is more powerful than mental and emotional subjectivity.
- Little distinctions can make a huge difference.
- It is awareness that allows the ordinary to become extraordinary!
- In the hands of an inspired artist, a worthless lump of clay becomes a work of art.

"Life isn't about finding yourself."
Life is about creating yourself."
—George Bernard Shaw

CHAPTER THREE

The Game of Life

The real victory lies in conquering yourself! By awakening an awareness of our true Self—the Soul—we have the potential to eliminate all fears, limitations, and suffering, and experience the life we are born to live!

Designed with Purpose

All human beings want happiness, but many do not know how to obtain it. Most people do not even realize that there is work to be done and a discipline to be followed. They think that, just because they are here on earth, they need only to eat, sleep, earn a living, and bring children into the world and they will automatically be happy. But animals do pretty much the same things, so what is the difference? We have a higher purpose.

If you want happiness, you must go out and start looking for the elements that nourish it. These elements belong to the inner world, so that is where you have to look for them. Once you understand them and have greater insight, you will have the power to create and achieve your dreams.

Realization
Think of Life and Love as verbs rather than nouns!

Life as an Action Sport!

To see life as a game is to recognize that it is definitely an action sport, so get in the Game!

The action sport of life requires conscious participation in the Game. You must learn to be action-oriented; let your actions be guided by common sense, intuition, and wisdom. Nowadays we see so many men and women drift dissatisfied through life, more as spectators than as participants. We can easily observe this when we look at the state of our world today; the outside world is a collective reflection of our inner world. To remedy and resolve our inner feelings of unhappiness and dissatisfaction, each of us needs to learn to be a conscious director of our life. We need to express purposeful and definite thoughts and actions from our own life center. *The time is now* to give up old estimates and beliefs of who and what we are and accept new possibilities. If we want to make a difference in this world, we first need to find the courage and commitment to make a difference in our own life. If we were to begin to use all available means, including our natural abilities, to overcome every obstacle in our path, we would quickly develop our INNERPOWER and discover more about who we already are!

It is only by *being* and *doing* that everything in the Game of Life becomes a reality and a living experience. Spectators may "know" exactly which play to make, but unless they are out on the field *being* a player and *doing* what a player should be doing, they do not have a real understanding of the situation. The gap between knowing and doing, for the majority, is very wide. Many people have trouble transforming their knowing into doing because they are always waiting—for permission from others or from themselves—until they feel happy or motivated, or until they no longer have feelings of fear or self-doubt. Waiting for other people and circumstances to change so that your own life will change is likely to be a very long wait—probably a lifetime of waiting.

> *Realization*
> To be alive at this time of accelerated human evolution is both an honor and a privilege. The time is now to become an active and influential force in your life, to be a conscious player in the Game of Life!

Be a Player!

How difficult is it to be a spectator? How difficult is it to be a skeptic or critic? A skeptic never loses, never fails, yet criticizes everyone else. I always encourage constructive doubt in the form of intelligent questioning; this is very productive as long as we base the conclusion on tests and personal experience. However, many skeptics are caught in a vicious circle; they are so skeptical that they do not really try, and because they do not try, they never see results and therefore remain skeptical. How many streets and buildings are named after skeptics? And why is it that there are so many people up in the stands watching the Game of Life instead of playing? Perhaps because it's easy?

In many ways, it is more difficult and frustrating to be a spectator, to watch a game in which you play no active role and therefore have no control in the final outcome. Many spectators feel as though they are actually playing the game, and many take it very seriously, some of them much too seriously. In today's world, we witness this more than ever as people's lives and happiness revolve around sporting events. Some spectators seem to live vicariously through the players rather than play their own game, and as a result they procrastinate or escape from playing the game of their own life. Have you ever noticed how bored a player looks when not playing? Once you have been a player and have had a taste of the action, although you appreciate the fans, you have no desire to be a spectator. A player thrives on the challenges and pressures of playing and is proud of the scars because they symbolize that injury is a part of the risk of playing and of daring to live life to its fullest.

> ## *Realization*
> Life is an action sport, not a spectator sport!

An Important Secret of Life

Your time is far too valuable to be only a spectator! You must learn to abandon your fears and imaginary limitations and get in the game. If you remain idle without doing something useful, your mind thinks scattered and random thoughts and wastes its energy. Many good thoughts die because they are not brought into action. Many people do not understand the value of energy and waste it carelessly. The individual who is successful, creative, and dynamic knows how to bring all their good and creative thoughts into action, giving form to their creative thinking process.

Realization
It's difficult getting into the spiritual swing of things when we are plagued by the adverse thoughts of doubt and fear from an untrained mind.

Of course, there are times to cheer our teammates on, just as long as we do not spend our lives up in the stands! I believe it is easier to cheer others on when we have our own game to play—when we are playing our role in the Game of Life.

Look at what it means to be a player in the Game of Life

PLAYER	SPECTATOR
Create	React
Cause	Effect
Gets paid to entertain	Pays to be entertained

To be a player in the Game of Life is to consciously be the cause, with the goal of creating a purposeful life; this requires a lot of work, energy, and discipline. To be spectators, on the other hand, is to be the effect, reacting to the players' game. Ironically, whether we participate or not, we are always the cause—the creator—because the *choices* we make in our lives determine and demonstrate whether we choose to be a player or a spectator.

Which would you rather be?

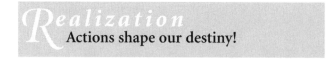

Realization
Actions shape our destiny!

Moving from "Get" Consciousness to "Give" Consciousness

The next step to being a player is to learn to be a giver rather than a taker—to progress from selfishness to selflessness! The people who are happiest in this world are those who are doing something for others, whether they are serving and making a difference for their family, their neighbor, their community, or their country. Yet most people define success according to how much they can "get." I believe a big reason for the increase in low self-worth and self-esteem that many people suffer from is the effect of a society that teaches people that "success" is to go out there and "get." With this attitude, we deny ourselves the pleasure of giving unconditionally and without expectation. Each of us has probably experienced feeling selfish or even guilty for feeling so good inside when helping others, yet nothing could be more natural. The gift is in the giving! When we return to the "Give" consciousness, everyone will benefit and the spirits of the world will be uplifted. Recognize that we are here to *serve* each other so as to serve God! Being in the service business, or game, we have to have a service attitude!

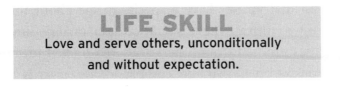

LIFE SKILL
Love and serve others, unconditionally and without expectation.

A Game of Giving and Receiving

Some people give too much because they have trouble receiving; they do not want to be a bother to anyone. This is selfish as well because they are now denying those who love them the pleasure of giving to them. Are you one of these people? It may help you to think of life as action, self-expression, giving. Realize that it is as necessary to give in order to live happily, as it is to breathe in order to stay alive. To receive from within or without and manifest what has been received is the natural way of life. To receive without giving or to give without receiving is to make life static and empty. We must open our hearts to both giving and receiving, and often we must give what we feel we need most, because invariably what we give comes right back to us. So whether it's money or a smile, give and receive with grace and gratitude!

Spiritual virtues have a special magic about them. When we cultivate them within our personality, similar qualities proceed from others and are directed towards us. For example, if you are compassionate towards others, compassion from an external source comes to you in a time of need.

Take a moment and use your breath as an analogy. Take a deep breath and feel the energy flowing inward for your body to use. Hold your breath so that your body can work with it, then exhale and give it away. Now do it again, only this time I would like you to imagine that you are inhaling pure love. Hold your breath and feel the love spreading throughout your body, healing and energizing every cell, then give that pure love away, back to where it came from. This is Life! Recognize that the inhalation and exhalation represent the dualities of life. Both are essential and of equal importance.

The Secret to Living Is Giving!

To receive more, we must give out what we have received. If we hold back, stagnation will follow and we will be like a wheel that generates power from water and suddenly, of its own volition, begins to withhold the water it is using. The wheel will soon find itself unproductive and sitting in inert water. It is only when the water is allowed to flow freely that it is of value and the wheel is able to create power.

As creative beings, we must express and give life to our ideas before we can receive their benefits. We must also allow and encourage fellow HUMANS IN TRAINING, our teammates, to do the same, so they can grow and develop as we do.

LIFE SKILL
Finding ways to make other people's days

*"Some of us go fishing all our lives
without realizing it is not fish we are after."*
—Henry David Thoreau

A Shift in Perspective

Action is important; however, action alone is not enough —it must be well directed with common sense, intuition, and wisdom. Many people swim upstream their whole life without being aware of it because they do not take their heads out of the water long enough to look! They have nothing to compare their lives to, so they just live life, work hard, and hope for the best. Then, when they experience the loss of a loved one, or perhaps a heart attack or cancer, there is a shift in perspective, a sense of urgency to live life more fully and consciously; they are now ready to be a player in the Game of Life.

I believe we all have times and experiences in our lives that change us by changing our perspective, turning points where we can never go back to being the person we were before no matter how much we may want to or how hard we may try. In fact, I believe this happens to us all the time; we need only to observe and be more aware.

Learning to Pay Attention

When I was eighteen years old, I first began to understand that daily life is more than it seems. I was away from home playing hockey and going to school. Life was sending me clear messages in the form of headaches, emotional instability, and problems concentrating. One morning I got up to go to school and passed out cold when coming out of the shower. I spent three days unconscious in the hospital until I was flown by helicopter to another hospital, where emergency surgery was performed. I awoke with half my head shaved and a tube extending from my brain to my stomach. I remember being at a neurological center about a week later, when the neurologist told me that I was lucky to be alive and even luckier not to be permanently brain-damaged. The doctor told me I would never play sports again and told my parents, "Let him do whatever he wants. He won't be with us for very long."

Wake-up Call

I find it amazing how we can have a life-changing experience and yet have a tendency to go back to what we were doing before. Although I should have recognized that life was giving me a vigorous wake-up call, I tried to go back to my old way of life by attending university and playing hockey. When the team doctors heard of my operation, they pulled me off the ice and demanded that I get permission from my neurologist to play. Of course, he flatly refused, so if I wanted to keep playing, my only option was to sign waiver forms. Then, during my first practice after I returned, I got a slap shot in the head, a concussion, and three stitches. Talk about being slow to take a hint!

Not yet ready to surrender to the message that life was literally hitting me over the head, I continued to play hockey. However, I began to realize that it no longer satisfied me as it once had; I was confused and frustrated, and I wanted answers to some of life's tough questions. I wanted to know the meaning and purpose of life and the reason why I was here. At the age of eighteen, I felt as though I was going through a mid-life crisis!

I began by asking questions, questions such as—

- What makes a difference in the quality of people's lives?
- What has changed my perspective so that some people who once seemed to have so much, now seem to have so little?
- What is the common denominator of success?
- What is true success?
- What is my purpose and role in life?
- Why do some people with every advantage do so little, while some with barely a chance do so much?

The most important question to me was—

- What is the one thing that I can work on, that will make everything else fall into place?

Wrapping versus Gift

At this point, hockey was just a game, and my true life journey was just beginning. I began to look for answers. I started by reading lots of books and getting bits and pieces here and there. As I searched for answers and my frustration and impatience deepened, it suddenly dawned on me that hockey was only the wrapping, and I was forgetting about the many gifts inside. I never had a deep passion for the game, although I did enjoy my role as a goaltender; however, I always felt that I was put on this earth to do more than stop hockey pucks, there had to be more—a deeper purpose to life. Why was I so afraid to discover my true purpose in life? And did I really want to know? I questioned myself on what it was about hockey that kept me playing all those years. I came to realize that my real passion all along was the teaching and speaking associated with hockey that I got to do, for I not only played, but taught as well. In teaching, what I really enjoyed was the *process* of developing the system to effectively pass on the knowledge to eager and curious students, and then watching them improve in their performance. I recognized not only a gift and passion for teaching, but also for taking something complicated and creating an efficient and practical system to help others learn. Personally, I also recognized that I enjoyed the competition as an opportunity to test my abilities and skills. I also appreciated the focus and the discipline that sports demanded, the importance of having goals, and having a reason to wake up in the morning.

Furthermore, I recognized that hockey was like meditation for me. Every day when I stepped onto the ice, I would focus on the game and everything else would simply fade away from my mind. My attention would become single-mindedly concentrated as I entered the "zone." Then, whenever I stepped off the ice, my mind would go out of control and become preoccupied with a constant stream of all of life's unanswered problems and questions. It was the need for freedom from my restless mind that acted as a trigger for my spiritual quest. Slowly, I came to realize that all my life, I had been focusing on the wrapping, the game of hockey itself, while the real gift—the teaching and speaking—had been inside all along. Now life was steering me into a new direction, opening my eyes to my soul's purpose through my newly discovered gift. Now I needed to refine these gifts, so that I could offer my very best to the world. If only it were that easy!

Realization
Meditation comes in many forms.

The Light Begins to Dawn

During my initial search for answers, I tried skydiving, bungee jumping, fire-walking, defensive knife fighting, and more. Anything death-defying and borderline crazy, I did it. Although these experiences were exciting and fun, I was still the same person inside; no real changes were taking place, and I was not finding the answers I was looking for. One day it finally struck me that what I was really after is called inner power—inner peace or peace of mind—and not "outer power," "outer peace", "peace" of car, "peace" of business, "peace" of relationship, or "peace" of anything else, and especially not "chaos" of mind, which is how I felt. I now see very clearly that all along I had been looking for answers in all the wrong places—no wonder I was so frustrated! It finally dawned on me that the hunger of the human spirit for answers to life's fundamental questions can never be satisfied with scholastic knowledge or physical efforts.

LIFE SKILL
Seeing the many gifts of life by looking deeper, beyond the wrapping.

I also felt frustrated by the seminars that I had attended because most were focused on changing behavior and habits, instead of changing the cause of the behavior and habits. No wonder I kept falling back to my old ways! Finally, I came to the realization that consciousness is the cause, and as we raise our consciousness, our habits and behavior naturally change. As spiritual and creative beings, to focus on raising our consciousness, we need to exercise at our spiritual and creative levels. As our consciousness is elevated, new behavior and habits are born, naturally replacing the old. Furthermore, I came to realize that consciousness is the cause of our behavior and habits, and to a large degree our circumstances, and we are the creator of consciousness. Does this not make us powerful?

Realization
With power comes responsibility; with responsibility comes power!

Life as a Team Sport

A team is a group of individual players who are committed to developing their full potential, as well as that of their teammates, for the good of the whole.

Fortunately for all of us, we are not playing the Game of Life alone. The desire for true knowledge burns alike in the hearts of all human beings. From this moment, I suggest that we begin to see each other as *teammates* in the Game of Life, rather than as competition or the enemy.

HUMANS IN TRAINING—we are all playing on the same team! It is a great privilege to know that, in this world we have more in common with each other than we could possibly have differences, and that we are connected in ways we do not yet fully understand.

We all have the same Coach, we all play in the same arena—the arena of daily life; we all experience life through a physical body, with our individual strengths and weaknesses; and we all share the embarrassments and humility of the human experience! We are playing this Game of Life together, whether we recognize it or not, and each of us is strengthened by the combined effort of the whole team.

When I say we are not alone, I am referring not just to other people, but also to the Universe as a whole. We are never alone or without guidance, never without opportunities or choices. So let's take advantage of this!

Realization
As a part of the Universe, each of us plays an essential role in it.

Teammates for Life

To see others as *teammates* is to gain the insight into humankind's deepest truth—that we are all One and equal, but at different stages of progression. Until we gain full insight into this deepest truth, we will always tend to view others as competitors and not as teammates. Because we are all One and equal, we play by the same rules—rules set up by our Coach and Creator—which apply equally and impartially to each of us. It is then up to us: we can choose to ignore these rules and suffer, or we can choose to learn and apply them and thereby smooth out the self-made problems and obstacles on our path in Life.

When I say not to see others as the competition, I do not mean not to be competitive, but to play as a teammate with the intention of helping your fellow players grow. Compete not to "beat" others or feel you have to "hate" anyone in order to play. Compete instead for the pure thrill and joy of it, using the competition as a means to test yourself and uncover your strengths and weaknesses; use your performance as a measure of the level at which you are playing. Competition can be a very positive, motivating force because it can teach us to value our abilities more deeply, and can lead to an appreciation and greater respect for the capabilities of others. By playing your best, you inspire those around you to do the same. Unfortunately, because competition is often the way to success and power in business, politics, and education, we are taught to compete against others instead of with them. When competition becomes combat, it loses its power, and sometimes we do not even like the person we have become in order to win. This type of competition creates pressure and disharmony in our minds and hearts, upsetting the natural balance of our lives. So get competitive with yourself by raising your standards, and see how much you can do for the benefit of the team. Being competitive with yourself also means setting higher standards that are consistent with your values, goals, and life purpose, and not compromising or lowering those standards for anyone.

Realization
Amateurs compete with other people; professionals compete with themselves!

As with any team, we must work independently on ourselves, as well as interdependently within a team, in order to help accelerate the growth and evolutionary process for everyone. It serves no purpose to criticize or judge our fellow teammates; it is far better to learn from and help each other for the good of the team.

Realization
Perhaps it is time to revise the saying "I'll take care of you and you take care of me," to "I'll take care of me for you, and you take care of you for me."

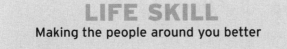

As Humans In Training, We Are a Family and a Team

In some ways, a team is like a family. However, it is interesting to recognize that sometimes teammates are kinder to each other than family members are. Why do you think that is? Perhaps it is because team members have a common objective—they are all trying to win the same game. Team players also realize they cannot do it all alone—they need their teammates!

Teammates help each other to win the game; each person plays a key role to assure the success of the team. They also have several obligations: to continue to improve personally; to encourage and help fellow teammates do the same; to know and understand the rules of the game; and, of course, to understand the system and game plan. A big difference in the Game of Life is that we have no authority to demand that others play at a specific level. We must maintain high expectations for ourselves and live as an example, while learning to support and respect the journey of each teammate.

There is no single path that leads to the realization of the Oneness of all life. Each soul has to walk its own path. However, all paths lead to the same destination. Great progress will take place as we shift our consciousness from competition to co-operation!

Embrace All of Humanity

As HUMANS IN TRAINING, we are like a family in that we are all connected within the human family. As a family and a team, we share several common objectives, especially to be winners in the Game of Life and to discover what that truly means. To be a part of something bigger than ourselves—in this case the human family—we are required to think on another level and to recognize that we are part of several teams: our spouse and family, coworkers, friends, society, nation, and our world as a whole. An important point to note is that as a team, we do not have to agree with, or even like, all our teammates because we do not consciously select them ourselves; however, we must learn to respect them. We can choose to focus on what we have in common and value and learn from our differences, and, most importantly, we can choose to commit to playing our very best and to fulfilling our obligations so that our team has a greater chance of winning.

Realization
A truly spiritual understanding among people and nations is urgently needed!

"An eye for an eye makes the whole world blind."
—Gandhi

The World as a Single Community

No longer can we think of ourselves as separate from the other peoples and cultures of the world, especially with modern modes of travel, communications, satellites, and particularly with our global environmental concerns. We desperately need the *spiritual maturity* to understand each other and to get along. Two great weaknesses of human nature, *prejudice* and *small-mindedness,* must be eliminated in order to move forward. Much war, suffering, and destruction will be prevented if we no longer emphasize differences and learn to love all without distinction or prejudice. Timeless truths of kindness, love, honesty, sincerity, and compassion are principles that will remain the same for ages to come!

Realization
Recognize the same Spirit within us all, blind to race, color, or gender.

As I mentioned earlier, it is the spiritual dimension of life that is the most universal and unifying dimension of all. Unfortunately, we are living in a time in which we experience war in the name of God. I am often asked about the difference between religion and spirituality. I believe in them both. There are many different paths to climb the same mountain, yet when you reach the top, the view is the same! The substance of all religions consists in the achievement of inner freedom; however, religion has a tendency to build an idol and separate people by instilling the fear of God and recognizing their way as the only way. Religion also often views God as separate from the individual and believes a mediator is necessary for higher attainment. Spirituality focuses on building the *ideal* and *uniting* people through a universal love for God. *Spiritual maturity* is the understanding that we are all part of one Spirit, which exists not only outside of us, but also, and more importantly, *within* every human being. All spirituality has self-understanding, self-discipline, and self-transcendence at its core. When we realize the true meaning of religion, which is to know God, we realize that God exists equally and impartially in all of us. INNERPOWER is designed to inspire those of all faiths, to reveal the essential unity of all world religions.

> *Realization*
> True spirituality fulfills our universal needs through direct personal experience of God, recognizing that the kingdom of Heaven is within.

A Spiritual Solution

You are a member of the worldwide human race! A citizen of the world! We can build a better world upon a foundation of deeper understanding, friendship, mutual support, respect, and unselfishness, by choosing to focus on life, not death; construction, not destruction; and love, not hate. Think for a moment of how the world would be different if the same money, time, and energy spent on destruction and separation were instead used for the purpose of construction and integration. We could easily remove the slums of the world, eradicate hunger, and give every person a better life! The time is now! We can rebuild our world one soul at a time.

Question:
Are you part of the construction crew or part of the wrecking crew?

"A house divided against itself cannot stand."
—Jesus

The above quote says it best. Think of this house on both an individual and a global level—our individual house of Mind, Heart, Strength, and Soul, and the international house of all humanity.

Realization The time has come! We must begin to think and act as One; we must come together and play like a team because we are a team!

Life Is a Partnership

Life is a partnership—A cooperative TEAM effort!

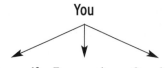

A most important point is the understanding that life is a partnership, and that all relationships are built on *love* and *trust*! They do not evolve and grow on their own or by accident. As HUMANS IN TRAINING, the key is to build and develop each of these relationships and understand their connection to each other and to our overall quality of life and happiness.

Success in business and success in life come down to two things—people and our relationships. We must first build a relationship with ourselves and with our Creator. As we do this, our relationships with others fall naturally into place. Recognize that it is most important to get along with yourself in order to get along in this world. If we cannot get along with or love ourselves, how can we expect to get along with and love others? Think of people you know who are unhappy with themselves and are experiencing difficulties in relationships with others—personal, family, work, and spiritual. It is difficult to truly love or respect anyone or anything if you do not love and respect yourself. We need only to look at the lack of respect that is shown to our environment, our teammates from all walks of life, our Creator, and ourselves to reflect this lack of understanding.

Why do so many relationships fall apart? We can come up with a lot of reasons, but these are only symptoms of the underlying causes—neglect and lack of attention!

> *Realization*
> **All relationships are like a fire that needs to be tended to maintain its life.**

As we consciously choose to be team players, we have an obligation to know and understand ourselves, to know and understand our teammates, to know and understand our Creator, and to improve each of these relationships. However, our prime obligation is to know and understand ourselves because it all starts with us! As we fulfill our role in life, everything else falls into place. We can raise the consciousness of our world one person at a time!

T E A M
Together Everyone Achieves More

1. What was (is) the greatest team you've ever been a part of?
2. What made (makes) it such a great team?
3. How did (do) you feel being part of the team?
4. What did (do) you contribute to the team?
5. What did (do) you receive from the team?
6. In a sentence or a phrase, how would you describe the mind-set of the team? Where did that mind-set come from?

Off the Bench and into the Game!

Like any game, life can be a great challenge, and that is exactly why we should enjoy it! We do not enjoy playing a game that is too easy or lacking in competition, do we? We enjoy the challenges and appreciate the victory of overcoming.

As a team player, we have a responsibility to ourselves, our teammates, and our Coach to fulfill our role in order to assure the success of the team. Others can inspire us, and conversely, by being an example ourselves, we can be helpful to others and be a source of inspiration and strength to them. Life is challenging enough. We have a choice to try to play all alone and attempt to do everything ourselves, or we can surrender and live life as we are meant to—with the support, respect, and love of our teammates and Coach. We are not alone! Let's begin today to work in harmony with our teammates and our Coach, unafraid to ask them for help, so that we can work together to be winners in the most important game of all.

The Art of Daily Living.

To succeed in any discipline demands training and strategy. Daily life is no exception! Most people struggle through life because they are at war inwardly, while also "battling" daily life. How many people are consciously training for daily life? As we begin training on both the inner and outer levels, we gradually make peace within, and our lives become an exciting journey as we realize who and what we really are.

"When there is no enemy within, the enemy outside us can do us no harm."
—African Proverb

The Goose Story

Next fall, when you see geese heading south for the winter, flying along in "V" formation, you might consider what science has discovered about why they fly that way. As each bird flaps its wings, it creates uplift for the bird immediately following. By flying in a "V" formation, the whole flock adds at least 70 percent more flying range than would be possible if each bird flew on its own.

People who share a common direction and sense of community can get where they are going more quickly and easily because they are traveling on the thrust of one another.

When a goose falls out of formation, it suddenly feels the drag and resistance of trying to go it alone and quickly gets back into formation to take advantage of the lifting power of the bird in front.

If we have as much sense as a goose, we will stay in formation with those who are headed the same way.

When the head goose gets tired, it rotates back in the wing and another goose flies point.

It is sensible to take turns doing demanding jobs, whether people working together, or geese flying south.

Geese honk from behind to encourage those up front to keep up their speed.

What do we say when we honk from behind?

Finally—and this is important—when a goose gets sick or is wounded by a gunshot and falls out of formation, two other geese fall out with the fallen goose and follow it down to lend help and protection. They stay with the fallen goose until it is able to fly or until it dies. Only then do they launch out with another formation to catch up with their group.

If we have as much sense as a goose, we will stand by each other like that.

Unknown Source

The Game of Life

- Life is an action sport, not a spectator sport!
- Actions shape our destiny!
- A gift is not a gift until it is given away.
- Meditation comes in many forms.
- With power comes responsibility; with responsibility comes power!
- As a part of the Universe, each of us plays an essential role in it.
- Amateurs compete with other people; professionals compete with themselves!
- A truly spiritual understanding among people and nations is urgently needed!
- Recognize the same Spirit within us all, blind to race, color, or gender.
- All relationships are like a fire that needs to be tended to maintain its life.

*"Everything that happens to
you is your teacher.
The secret is to learn to sit at the feet
of your life and be taught."*
—Polly Berends

The Law of Life

The Law of Life is to refine the nature of humankind until we are a complete and perfect expression of life itself. As Humans In Training, we are driven to find perfection. This is our Soul nature struggling to perfect itself. Each of us is fueled by the need that comes from deep within us to achieve this single goal.

Life Lessons

Because we are spiritual beings, life lessons are spiritual lessons; we experience them to help us learn to understand our responsibility, role, and purpose. When we use life's experiences as our teacher, we learn the true nature of the world and our part in it. Those experiences become valuable lessons, we appreciate them, and they serve us for our highest good.

As we begin to explore the Game of Life together, I would like you to begin to think of daily life as a giant feedback mechanism—our "training ground." Here, day-to-day living is guaranteed to teach us everything we need to grow and evolve, by continually testing us, teaching us, and strengthening us. Take a moment to reflect on how our body acts as a perfect feedback mechanism that always provides direct and accurate information. When we exercise, we get results in direct proportion to our efforts, no more, no less. When we abuse or neglect our body, we become sick or feel pain—clear feedback signals that are the natural expressions of the body. Our body is so perfectly designed that it also lets us know when there is any disharmony or underdevelopment on other levels, mental, emotional, or spiritual, so that we can make the necessary changes within. Our body is the warehouse for our thoughts and feelings, and simply cannot tell a lie. Whatever we feel in our body is our truth. Disease is our body telling us that something is wrong. As we begin to see ourselves as students of life, we must make an important connection—just as our body acts as a physical feedback mechanism, life itself is a giant feedback mechanism communicating with us all the time. This connection creates an awareness that we cannot fool ourselves or get away with anything on the physical level, and more importantly, that we cannot fool the Universe or get away with anything in life on any level! Life is a constant observer, so it serves no purpose to lie, cheat, or be dishonest because the Universe knows our intentions. We may try to bend the rules or get away with something, but eventually we learn from the consequences that we are held *accountable* for every thought and every action. A morally sound life places us in a position of strength because it activates the spiritual resources that allow us to play the Game of Life more effectively.

Compare the world situation to the human body. When the cells are healthy, the organs are healthy; when the organs are healthy, the whole body is filled with vitality. However, if something is wrong with the cells, then the health of the entire body is affected. In the same way, the stability and health of our world as a whole depends on the health of society and of each individual.

> **Realization**
> We often fail to get relief from disease because we treat the disease and not our ignorance that has caused it! The way of escape is through wisdom.

Life Is a School—Growth Is the Name of the Game

As HUMANS IN TRAINING, each of us is enrolled in a full-time school and daily life is our classroom. As we walk consciously on the road to self-discovery, we need to recognize that human development is an ongoing refining process, one that never ends. We can only learn more—never less—and therefore, we can only get better when we put in the effort. Growing is the most important and essential endeavor that a human being can undertake because the growth we attain in our search for Self-knowledge is something that nobody can ever take away from us. This growth and understanding strengthens our foundation and sustains us through any and all difficulties.

We have no choice but to evolve and grow; life is a school and as its students, we are in different grades of learning, whether we are aware of it or not, whether we are participating or not. The difference, however, lies in the speed of evolution; each Soul progresses according to its individual efforts. Conscious participation quickens the process, whereas unconscious participation slows it down because we will have to repeat the lesson until it is finally learned.

> *Realization*
> **Spirit never judges us; it only gives us opportunities to balance, learn, and grow!**

A Higher Purpose

Life provides us with endless opportunities for introspection and self-understanding, which are essential preliminaries to self-transformation. Eventually, we do learn from the consequences of our actions or inaction. I have always found it amazing that if we do not learn, we can be sure that the same life lessons will return again and again, and with each return, the consequences will be tougher, until we finally do get the lesson. We have all experienced this process working on all levels, personally, professionally, in our relationships with others, when identifying our role and purpose, and of course spiritually. We attract the same type of people or circumstances over and over until the lesson is finally learned. Would you agree that this is a sign of a pretty amazing and intelligent Universe? And would you agree with me that this is a very clear signal of a *higher purpose* for all of us? Is this not proof that this higher sense of purpose is indeed an inherent faculty of all HUMANS IN TRAINING? Sometimes it can feel as though life is being hard on us, even punishing us at times; however, it is essential to recognize and trust that what we are experiencing is for our highest good and purpose. This is only school; we have come here to go through all of life's experiences and to learn from them. Pain is a prod to remembrance! The Universe is designed to help us remember who we are in truth. The principal lesson we are expected to learn is that we are the same One. When we forget why we are here, that is when our troubles begin!

Question:

Have you recognized that there is a force and power you can call upon for health, happiness, and spiritual awakening?

> *"The game of life is a game of boomerangs; our words and deeds return to us with astounding accuracy."*
> —Florence Scovel Shinn

Life as Our Coach

As you begin to think of your life in terms of a partnership, it may help to think of the Universe or God as not only your partner, but also your very own personal Coach, always bringing to your attention what is most important for you to work on in your life. A coach will always be teaching, testing, and helping us to realize our full potential, as well as disciplining us when we need it. In order to play our best, we need to learn how to *listen* to and *trust* our Coach, as well as to understand the process of life itself. As we do, our game naturally improves. I am sure that sometimes many of you find that life can be a very stern teacher. This happens only when we miss life's lessons, so it is up to us to be aware of them. We must learn to see past successes and failures, our own and those of others, as our university studies for success! Our education is never-ending and everyone, and every circumstance becomes our teacher. We can learn just as much valuable information from watching others' failures as we can from observing their accomplishments. By paying attention to what is going on inside and around us, we can learn life's lessons more quickly and less painfully. The more we play, the quicker we grow and progress through the opportunities and experiences that Life sends our way.

> *R*ealization
> Within our daily activities is hidden the meaning of life.

Life as a Practice Game

As part of the inherent urge of the Universe towards progression and evolution, every problem in need of a solution is an opportunity imposed upon us by life itself. A problem—or better, an opportunity—is only a statement of certain conditions and serves as a means of growth for the individual, company, society, or the world as a whole. For example, summer and winter are not two things but phases of one nature. Winter is as essential to the growth of vegetation as is summer; they depict two phases of a single process. When life is seen in this way, all unpleasantness disappears and everything becomes a practice game. Recognize that practice is about *progress*, about working to extract the lesson contained in every experience.

LIFE SKILL
Learn the lesson contained in every experience.

"The basic difference between an ordinary man and a warrior is that a warrior takes everything as a challenge, while an ordinary man takes everything as either a blessing or a curse."
—Carlos Castaneda

Realization
Life is a matter of progress determined by the kind and quality of our expression.

We need to use circumstances as aids to achieve more rapid progress and as a means of discovering the hidden powers and possibilities within us. Any escape from our problems, on any level, is not an escape from life but a delay in our progress and a source of further pain and obstacles.

Realization
We are designed to be challenged!

Life as a Preparation Process

As a result of my brain surgery, I felt an intense urgency to discover and learn—something that is key to growing. Adversity—or, as my dad would say, "character building"—is a reminder to move our lives in certain directions, to learn life's lessons, and to develop specific skills necessary to fulfill our purpose. So what do I mean by "life is a preparation process"? Everything that has ever happened to us in our lives—the people and circumstances we have attracted to ourselves and the lessons learned from these experiences—is life's way of preparing us to achieve and fulfill our individual purpose, as well as our purpose as HUMANS IN TRAINING. When we begin to recognize this, we discover that everything happens for a reason and serves us, whether we understand it at the time or not. This is the key! We do not have to immediately understand why; we must simply recognize and trust life as a preparation process and know that everything will unfold at the right time—there is a right season for everything. In this way, we can become not only better listeners and learn the lessons more quickly, but we can also begin to think in terms of a larger plan.

Question:

If life is a preparation process, what has life been preparing you for personally, professionally, and spiritually?

> *"We are not human beings*
> *having a spiritual experience.*
> *We are spiritual beings*
> *having a human experience."*
> —Teilhard de Chardin

Living Is Learning—Learning Is Living

Often in life we get caught up or distracted by the wrapping, making the mistake of thinking that this is all there is. Pain and adversity force us to look deeper, beyond the wrapping until we discover the gift. Let's face it, pain, adversity, and death are very effective means for the Universe to get our attention in order to urge us to grow and evolve to the next level—and it works! Without adversity, we would never evolve or discover our purpose because we would become complacent towards life. Life is a series of tests and trials until we have mastered all its important yet basic lessons. Therefore, it is quite normal for us to feel that our problems are endless because life is continually making sure that no stone of greed, dishonesty, fear, doubt, anger, or rejection is left unturned. It is constantly forcing us to confront our dark side until we learn to transform it into light. Every stage demands that we be courageous and brave. As children, we trusted life; we were naturally brave and courageous, and we continually explored new and different things. As we grow in understanding, we become more childlike! Life becomes simpler, and we enjoy the journey of our unique life unfolding.

Question:

Do you remember the very first time that you stopped living in the moment and started to doubt and question life?

We all have times or experiences in our lives when we say to ourselves, "why me?"—only to discover down the road exactly why. No matter how many times this may happen, we never seem to learn to trust the process; we keep questioning, and perhaps complaining, when changes occur. We have to learn to trust and have faith that everything plays a part for our highest good and purpose. When the going gets tough, there is no other reason; it is not a punishment, as many might believe, it is the Universe moving us forward and making us accountable for the choices we have made.

> *R*ealization
> Trusting the process of life empowers us to bounce back from adversity and to have the courage to take chances.

"This Doesn't Look Good."

When I was twenty-three, I began experiencing seizures during my sleep, as a side effect of the surgery. I was informed that this was common, caused from scarring on the brain. That same year, I decided to move to Vancouver for a fresh start. The seizures kept occurring, and after having six in a four-month period and experiencing some memory loss, I went to see a neurologist for help. He explained to me that a seizure is the equivalent of a concussion, which would explain the memory loss, and gave me medication to stop the seizures. The medication was known to have serious side effects, so I asked the neurologist what we could do to find out more about the *cause* of the seizures and work on that, because I did not want to take the medication for the rest of my life. He told me that the medication was the best he could do for me, so I began taking it, feeling that I had no other option.

Three weeks after my initial visit to the neurologist, I received a letter in the mail from the Motor Vehicle Commission, informing me that my driver's license had been revoked at the request of the neurologist. I had just started a new job, which required a car, and was in my second week of training. So, in just one morning, I lost my driver's license, my job, and my source of income. In addition, I had rent to pay, a brand new sports car under lease, and my health was not very good because I was adapting to the strong new medication and still recovering from the past seizures. I called the neurologist to ask him why he did not tell me he would be recommending the suspension of my driver's license so that I could have been prepared. His response shocked me; he said, "I didn't have to tell you, I am above the law."

Push Comes to Shove

I contacted several other neurologists for help in getting my license back, but I kept getting the same response; they would not challenge the other doctor's decision, even if they did not agree with it because they did not want to jeopardize their careers in any way. Finally, the sixth neurologist I consulted said he would help me. He began by contacting the neurological center where I had last been treated and learned that the doctors there were surprised to hear that I was still alive because I had been diagnosed with a mid-brain tumor and had been given only fifteen months to live—and that was five years earlier!

A Truly Unexpected Bonus!

The neurological center that had given me only fifteen months to live did not bother to find out more information about my injury or do any follow-up. My new neurologist, upon discovering that I was adopted, suggested contacting the adoption center to get my medical records. On the application was a question asking if I would be interested in meeting my biological mother. I had often thought that I would like to, if for no other reason than to say thank you for giving me life, but I had never gotten around to it. Well, I now had the time! A few weeks later, I received a letter in the mail with the medical records of my biological family. For the first time, I saw the physical description of my biological mother and father. The same letter also said that the adoption center was underfunded, and it would take four to five years to locate my biological mother, but if I were to send five hundred dollars immediately, they would do their best to shorten the waiting period to two years. Well, I did not need to meet her that badly, or so I thought.

Later that same day, I received a phone call from the adoption center. The woman asked me if I believed in coincidences. She informed me that my biological mother had just opened the file less than a year ago to make my medical information available. Not only that, but also my file and hers had ended up in the woman's office, which is one of seventeen locations, and both files were in her hands as we spoke! In fact, she had just got off the telephone with my birth mother!

The Plan Continues to Unfold

Coincidentally, I was leaving the next day to go to Montreal, where my sister was having her first baby. My biological mother, who lived in New Jersey, was visiting her family that weekend as well, only an hour away from Montreal! With the enthusiastic support and blessing of my adoptive parents, we arranged to meet for lunch. I was delighted to meet her. She was tall and slender with dark hair and blue eyes, just like me, and she even talked as fast as I did! I also learned that she had been the runner-up for Miss Teen Canada only seven months after giving birth to me, and she had been a model with a top modeling agency in New York for many years and had appeared on magazine covers all over the world. I was amazed at how the loss of my driver's license four weeks earlier had started a string of unusual events and synchronicities that ultimately reunited me with my biological mother! I have always been grateful that I did not give up after the fifth neurologist said no to my request to help me get back my driver's license, because it was the sixth neurologist whose initiative to contact the adoption center made this reunion possible.

Such a chain of coincidences is not all together uncommon; in fact, if we were all in tune and paying attention, we would witness many striking "coincidences" occurring in our own life.

Realization
Life always has a way of working itself out.

Trusting the Process of Growth

Understanding is a process of growth. In weight training, you cannot become stronger unless you continue to increase the resistance you work with. Adversity provides lessons and opportunities to grow and develop inner strength; it is all part of life's preparation process. People and circumstances challenge us in order to get our attention, reveal our weak areas, and force us to grow and change. Expressions such as, "with every adversity comes the seed of an equivalent or greater success" and, "as one door closes, another opens" have withstood the test of time because of their truthfulness. Many people never get to the success that awaits them because they do not persist long enough—because they do not understand this process. To get more consistent and tangible results in life, everyone must first understand the manifestation process, then consciously participate in it, and finally and most importantly, *trust* that the process of life will unfold and develop without any interference from our fears, doubts, or impatience.

LIFE SKILL
Trusting the process of our unique lives unfolding

Understand—Participate—Trust

It is very difficult to trust the process of life unfolding if we do not first understand what this process is all about. The perfect analogy is the garden. If we want to grow a garden of flowers, we must follow a certain procedure. If any of the steps within the procedure are missed, we are not likely to reap the rewards of the planting. Many people never give themselves a chance because they throw the seeds for the flowers they desire on the ground, and then hope that they will grow if it is meant to be.

The first step to achieving a garden of flowers is to prepare the soil. Then, in the right temperature and environment, we plant the specific seeds for the flowers we desire. Next, we provide the seeds with water and fertilizer to help nourish them for growth. After doing our part, we must trust that when the seeds are ready, they will sprout and eventually the flowers will bloom. Recognize that the first three steps are the responsibility of the gardener! In life, it is no different. We must first prepare a strong inner foundation. Then we plant the specific seeds for the goal we desire, in the right condition and environment suitable to our needs. Next, we nourish our seeds with specific training, persistence, discipline, and determination. After doing our part, we must simply trust that when the time is right, we will experience results in direct proportion to our preparation and conditioning and to the degree that serves our higher purpose.

A gardener understands that the soil is alive and will bring forth either weeds or flowers. We must recognize that the Universe is alive and will bring forth. If we wish to create a botanical masterpiece with our life, we must plant the seeds we want to harvest. If we want to harvest carrots, we must plant carrot seeds. In daily life, if we want love, we need to plant the seeds of love. If we want peace in the world, we must plant the seeds of inner peace. What seeds are you sowing in your life?

Realization
Each seed has the completed flower within itself!

Making the First Move

Our understanding of this process must also embrace the understanding that we are always in a partnership with life. To the extent that we do our part within this relationship with life, life shall do its part in its partnership with us by delivering to us the opportunities necessary to achieve our goals. Our contribution to Life as its partner is the responsibility that we take the *initiative* with the right *intentions.* It is always up to us, and never to others, to take the first, struggling step and make the first move. The first step is always to make the decision that we want to be a player in the Game of Life. Then we must find our purpose; many people spend a lifetime looking for it because there is nothing to lose and always something to complain about. Finding our purpose takes a lot of Soul-searching and Self-reflection, but once it is found, then what? That is the real challenge. This challenge may have to be addressed by taking such steps as quitting our job, moving to a new city or country, or letting go of a partner, whatever may be necessary when we are experiencing constant emotional turmoil and stress. The solution could also be to stay exactly where you are and to change *yourself.* Only you know deep down what the first step in the right direction is. It is different for everyone. Let your intuition and common sense guide you. Then have the *courage* to carry it out, no matter how faltering at first. Then you will find that there is another step for you to carry out, then another, each step increasing your strength and confidence.

When we do our part in our relationship with life, life rewards us. What are you communicating?

> **Realization**
> We have an inherent drive to do what we are here to do, and a fear and reluctance to do just that!

Many people spend their lives waiting for a sign, when all along it is the Universe that is waiting for them to take that first step. I love the analogy of a person standing in front of an unlit fireplace, freezing cold, holding a large bundle of wood. Instead of taking the first step in lighting up the fire with the wood, this person thinks, "Okay, fireplace, you give me some heat, then I'll put in some wood." It is impossible for this person to extract any warmth from the fireplace, for they have neglected to take the initiative to make a fire with the wood in their hands. Life works like the fireplace. Just as you have to take the first step in lighting up the fire with the wood in your hands, you have to take the first step in "lighting up" your life with all the resources and opportunities that life constantly sends your way. The old expression, "you can't steal second base and keep one foot on first" is an accurate reflection of the mind-set of many people. They will make an effort to steal second base only if they know for sure that they will arrive there safely. This is why it is so important that we understand the process and purpose of our lives unfolding, so we can continue to move forward on the right path with the understanding that we are not alone or without guidance.

> ## Realization
> To trust the process of life is to take that all-important first step without needing to have all the answers, and by operating on understanding, trust, and intuition.

Unfortunately, through past experiences, we accumulate doubts, fears, and other negative emotions. These negative emotions become deeply rooted within our psyche, and they interfere with our ability to trust our intuition, preventing us from advancing to the next level in the Game of Life. With greater self-awareness and understanding of our journey, we will have the courage to step forward into the seemingly unknown with greater confidence and faith.

Question:
Do you trust the process of your life unfolding?

Practice the Daily Lessons of Life

Think of life's lessons as steps up the mountain of success, each step laying the foundation for the step that is to follow. As we recognize and come to terms with the natural order of progression and purpose, we can work to uncover the lesson contained in every experience. Through ongoing *practice*, we can quickly detect the lesson contained in every experience, and with each discovery comes the opportunity to learn the lesson as soon as possible. As a result, our progress speeds up, enabling the Universe to send us more lessons on a higher level in the school of life.

> *Realization*
> We need to move beyond judging everything as either good or bad, and accept life's challenges as friends, teachers, and opportunities.

Law of Duality

This world is created through the law of duality; there are two sides to everything!—light and darkness, pleasure and pain, health and sickness, life and death, war and peace, positive and negative. Each human being has the *choice* to align their consciousness with one side or the other. Daily life will present us with a series of choices. Each of these choices involves giving up something we want for something else we want more. Every choice has consequences and teaches us something new about ourselves. Understanding this allows us to make conscious, rather than unconscious, choices in our life. Living harmoniously and making deliberate choices empowers us to become aware of life's plan and its lessons. When we express life in this way, we become our own best lesson book and teacher.

Life Definitely Builds Character!

Life is continually urging us towards the direction of fulfilling our purpose. It is constantly calling us to discover who we are and our gift to the world. It does this through the experiences and opportunities that it sends our way. As we become better listeners and pay attention to where life is guiding us, we can identify our purpose quickly and have fewer stumbling blocks to overcome.

Our fears and doubts often keep us in situations that are not for our highest good. We hear the call but do not have the courage and confidence to take the first step. The Universe will not plant a seed in our mind and heart without the ability to see it through. Only our limited conscious mind or other spectators will attempt to talk us out of it. As we progress along the journey of our life, we will experience that with each step forward in the direction of our purpose, the path will appear under our feet.

LIFE SKILL
Erasing doubt and fear from our consciousness and replacing them with faith and trust

A Refining Process

Life is a preparation process; it helps to also think of it as a *refining process*. Seen in this way, success is not an option; it is merely a matter of time before it is achieved. Therefore, what is normally viewed as a failure or a mistake, we HUMANS IN TRAINING see as a step closer to achieving success. So, are you willing to take as many steps as necessary until you succeed?

Achieving success is not only a refining process, but it also molds our character. The nature and identity of HUMANS IN TRAINING is a process of continual refinement. Think of how school is an ongoing learning process from grade one to college or university. Think of the stock market—sometimes up, sometimes down, but overall on the rise. Some companies make it and others don't. There can be a bull market and a bear market, but as a whole, the market is always growing. Similarly, the trend of HUMANS IN TRAINING is evolution; we are continuously growing and refining our character to reflect the image of our highest good within.

LIFE SKILL
Extracting the highest and best from every person and experience

Our character is formed by how we respond not only to life's successes, joys, and happiness, but also to its failures, disappointments, rejections, and the challenges of daily life. In any worthwhile endeavor, there are often going to be many adversities to overcome. In fact, we learn most about others and ourselves by the way that we respond to these adversities. Life will certainly make sure that we have endless opportunities to develop character—sometimes it feels like too many! How do you respond? Does failure or rejection control you, or does it inspire you? Do you take it personally? Are you easily dejected or depressed by life's tests and trials? Do you blame others for your life or the way you feel? Realize that you alone have the power to make changes in your life. The way your life is at this moment is a result of your very own current or past decisions or indecision. So if there is anything in your life that you are not happy with, do not sit back and wait for something to happen because that something that you are waiting for is you yourself. You are the solution to all of your life's problems.

Character Building

In society, do we not admire those who have had to fight and overcome many difficulties to achieve their success, often against all odds? How important is character in achieving goals? How important are tests and trials in building strength? It is easy to make the mistake of believing that rejection and failure are required to build strength; however, it is possible to build character in their absence by other means, such as working at building a strong will, determination, and perseverance.

Furthermore, if you believe failures and rejections are important for building character and inner strength, then you are choosing a very difficult path in the Game of Life, the path in which one constantly attracts failures and rejections. You can choose a much smoother path, an easier way—the way of Love.

> *Realization* The highest understanding of Love lies in its power to transform lives, restore health, and bring about a sense of total well-being.

Love is a powerful force that controls and rules everything, the controlling force we must cultivate within our own being. Ultimately, it is Love that we are all here to learn—to give and receive Love unconditionally and without expectation, and to appreciate, support, and respect ourselves, our teammates, and our world. For creatures who want to be loved and appreciated, we certainly go about fulfilling our desire in a curiously unfulfilling way. Instead of cultivating Love ourselves, we complain about not getting enough of it, search frantically for someone else to give it to us, and try to make ourselves more loveable by improving our looks or earning more money. The most effective way to get Love is to generate it yourself. By cultivating caring, loving feelings, you can actually provide yourself with the nourishment you desire. At the same time, by radiating those feelings outward towards others, you can touch their hearts and naturally bring out the same feelings in them. This creates a flow of Love that keeps circulating and building on itself.

> ## Realization
> **Love is the strongest magnetic force in the Universe.**

Support System

Life is supporting us in many ways. You may not feel this way because you simply have not been noticing. Often we resist and fight the process by worrying, lacking in faith or confidence, being impatient, or just by trying too hard. Life will support you; it is designed to do just that. So relax and trust. Surrender yourself to the Law of Life!

Resistance versus Surrender

To resist the Law of Life and attempt to live the way we may think life should be is to choose a difficult and lonely path. Resistance takes a lot of energy away from our spirit; everything is a fight and a struggle. As long as we resist a situation, it will stay with us; if we choose to run, it will follow us wherever we go or try to hide.

To surrender to the Law of Life is to recognize the order and purpose of our life, and to live and work in harmony with the support of the Universe. To surrender is not to give up, but rather, to give in, to free yourself from the weight you have been carrying your whole life. To let go of the struggle initiates a change of consciousness within. This change puts us in touch with the flow of life, and we experience a sense of *effortlessness* as we give in to a force greater than ourselves. As we surrender to a higher purpose, we feel that we are here to *serve*. We know that we are not alone as we experience divine guidance in our life, as well as the constant renewal of life energy that allows us to move forward. This is our freedom and birthright.

Realization
Like all power, InnerPower must have a nonresistant instrument to work through; we are that instrument!

Stress is our reaction to what we imagine to be wrong in our lives. Stress is not born from without, but rather from within our own nature, resulting from our interpretation—or rather misinterpretation—of an event. To have INNERPOWER is to be in control of both our actions and our reactions with a greater understanding and therefore trust of the process. I once held the belief that nothing of any value in life is going to be easy, because if it were easy, it would not have any value. As long as we are resisting in our life, this belief is true. It took a dear friend to bring this to my attention so I could see how false my belief was and how many of my struggles were self-imposed. Only when I became aware of how this belief was affecting my life could I exercise my power to change it.

What Is Your Purpose? Your Passion?

What have you naturally gravitated towards? What have you been led towards by experiences? What lessons have you realized from successes and failures? What special talents and skills have you acquired? What is it that, when you talk about it, uplifts your whole spirit so that others can feel your passion?

One of my favorite questions, which has been used by many in different forms, is simply: If you knew for a fact that you would be successful, what would you attempt to do? Most people are not able to answer this question because they have never thought in those terms. It requires reflection and sincere, deep, inner searching. One key to knowing that you have identified your purpose is when it feels right and you sense in your heart, mind, and Soul that it would be fulfilling. This search demands looking beyond the surface—the gift wrapping —to uncover the true gifts and lessons that life has been preparing you for. What do you enjoy doing that lifts your whole spirit and feels right on all these levels?

Realization
Passion + Uniqueness = Purpose

I will never forget my very first presentation to raise interest in my INNERPOWER seminar. I was given thirty minutes to share my approach and offer my program to thirty associates of a financial planning firm as a good investment of their time and money. I spoke from my heart and gave what I thought was a great talk and offered my course at an incredible price, just hoping to have some people to practice my ideas on. Not one person signed up! I went to the washroom so I could be alone. I was so pumped up and it felt so right inside that I just knew this was it! I was finally closer to my purpose, now I just had to get good at it! A year and a half later, that same company became one of my largest corporate clients!

The Courage to Surrender

Many people want to live "on purpose," but are they prepared to do the Soul-searching to get there? Furthermore, once they know what their purpose is, do they have the real courage to take that first step, that leap of faith to make it happen? Could this be why so many people are afraid to seek and materialize their future?

Question:
    Are you living in harmony with your purpose?

Realization
The universe holds us accountable and provides us with the feedback we need to fulfill our purpose.

We Control the Power

If we recognize life as a matter of progress, we must realize that progress presupposes the existence of the power of growth that exists within us. Just as a seed contains within itself the power to express its greatest purpose, we too, contain within ourselves the power to express our greatest accomplishment—life. No flower bursts into full bloom without an inner urge to grow, develop, and multiply. The power is already in the seed planted in the earth; we do not see what is going on within. As the seed must first burst its shell in order to grow, so must we burst our shell of limitations in order to grow.

Keep Forging Ahead

Life is a giant feedback mechanism revolving around a definite purpose and a plan. It is constantly preparing us to achieve and fulfill our purpose. However, it is up to us to be aware of the lessons and move in that direction. Sometimes we are moving in the other direction, consciously or not. But if we are mindful of our thoughts, emotions, and actions, we can never get lost. We are here to learn and grow. We will have trials and tribulations until all lessons are finally learned. Life will guarantee you that!

Realization
We can no longer deny the presence of an intelligent force pushing us progressively toward an expansion of consciousness.

Despite all trials and tribulations, life is much simpler when we learn to trust. There is a force and rhythm in life that comes to our assistance in the most unpredictable ways. It comes more often and in greater abundance when we demonstrate our faith and take that all-important first step!

The lesson we are here to learn is to harmonize our "outward" responsibilities with our "inner" search for God. *God is our center*, the strength that we need to carry out the duties that are assigned to us as part of our earthly schooling.

Realization We can understand the process but we cannot rush it! Life is a process of discovering our worth and the worth of all Humans In Training. We cannot *make* this happen, we can only *let* it happen.

"Watch your thoughts: they become words.
Watch your words: they become actions.
Watch your actions: they become habits.
Watch your habits: they become character.
Watch your character: it becomes your destiny."

—Tony Barrett

Old Parable

A hermit lived on the edge of a forest close to a small village. The villagers all thought he was a fool, for he spoke in paradoxes. His name was Jed. One day, Jed took in a stranger who was sick and nursed him back to health. In gratitude, the stranger gave him a horse. When the villagers heard what had happened, they all congratulated Jed.

"Jed, what good luck! What great fortune!"

"Who knows if it's good luck?" Jed responded. "Maybe it's bad luck."

"Bad luck," they laughed. "How can it possibly be that? You had no horse, now you have one. This is good luck!" *What a fool,* they thought, *he cannot even recognize good luck when it happens to him.*

Jed took his meager savings and bought a saddle. Then one day, the horse escaped and ran away.

"Oh, what bad luck!" the villagers said when they heard what had happened. "You now have a saddle and no horse."

"Who knows if it's bad luck? Maybe it's good luck," Jed responded cheerfully.

"Good luck?" they laughed. "There's no way this is good luck. This is a tragedy for you."

"Who knows?" said Jed.

Several days later, the horse mysteriously returned, bringing with him a couple of wild horses. Jed quickly led them into a corral. Word soon spread that he now had three horses. The villagers rushed to see for themselves.

"What good luck!" they said to Jed. "You now have three horses. You can sell two and keep one for yourself."

"Who knows if it's good luck?" Jed said. "Maybe it's bad luck that this has happened."

"Bad luck!" they laughed, unable to hide their pity for such a simple-minded fool.

One day while attempting to ride one of the wild horses, Jed was thrown and broke his leg.

"What bad luck!" the villagers said when they learned of the mishap.

"Who knows?" said Jed. "Maybe it's good luck that I broke my leg."

A week later an invading army stormed into the village and forcibly conscripted all the men who were in good health, but they did not take Jed because he had a broken leg.

It is an old parable, and the story goes on and on. The message is clear: Who knows what is good or bad luck?

"Any darn fool can make something complex;
it takes a genius to make something simple."
—Pete Seeger

The Law of Life

- Spirit never judges us; it only gives us opportunities to balance, learn, and grow!
- Within our daily activities is hidden the meaning of life.
- We are designed to be challenged!
- Life always has a way of working itself out.
- Each seed has the completed flower within itself!
- Accept life's challenges as friends, teachers, and opportunities.
- Doubt and fear must be erased from our consciousness and replaced with faith and trust.
- Love is the strongest magnetic force in the Universe.
- INNERPOWER must have a nonresistant instrument to work through.
- *Passion* and *Commitment* are the key ingredients in every success recipe.

"When we see everyone is a part of us,
that any criticism we make is self-criticism,
we will extend to ourselves an unconditional love
that will light the world."

—Harry Palmer

CHAPTER FIVE

A Perfect World

Within every seed is the perfect design and completed picture for its fulfillment and perfect self-expression.

Within every desire is the perfect design and completed picture for its fulfillment and perfect self-expression.

Within every human being is the perfect design and completed picture for our fulfillment and perfect self-expression.

We Are the Problem, Not Nature!

To achieve INNERPOWER, we must gain insight, understanding, and appreciation of the universal, natural laws that operate in the world we live in.

Understanding our world is acknowledging that you and I are part of an open, dynamic, and intelligent Universe, where conscious purpose underlies everything. It is the realization that every human being is created in an intricately organized body and that we are the architects of our own destiny. Most importantly, it is the knowledge of the true relationship that exists between our source and ourselves.

Realization
It is a perfect world because in our structured universe *laws of right behavior* are part of the universal order.

Rules of the Game

One of my favorite quotes is from Einstein, who once said, "God does not play dice with the Universe." In other words, our world is created in the most scientific and mathematically precise manner and is set up perfectly for us. Everything in the Universe operates according to laws—all that we see, smell, touch, taste, hear, and feel, as well as the laws that govern the movement of the earth, the number of days in a year, the cycle of the seasons, gravity, speed, sound, color, and genetics. There is an established order in the Universe, and only through aligning ourselves with that natural order can we hope for fulfilling results. Nature can work only with the material it has!

An established law in the Universe is unchangeable. It is so exact that at any moment, the position of any star or planet can be mathematically determined to the second. This balance is so perfect that there is no deviation—if just one molecule were out of place, we would no longer exist! When we think of it this way, we can easily recognize that all laws reign perfectly throughout the Universe—all things, from subatomic particles to huge galaxies, operate according to definite laws and principles.

> ## *Realization*
> All forces are governed by intelligence. If they were not, they could not produce such a well-planned universe.

Question:

Do you really think that you and I are the one exception in the entire Universe, our lives guided only by luck, chance, and coincidence?

We Are Not Above the Law

In our structured Universe, there can be no compromise or negotiating with exacting laws. Universal laws operate with impartial justice, regardless of individual beliefs, and serve as guidelines to help us learn through direct feedback. For example, the law of gravity is not concerned with whether or not you are skeptical! Nature is ready and willing to disclose her secrets to us. Her laws are revealed everywhere in the natural world, as well as within each of us. These laws apply equally and impartially to everything and everyone in the Universe.

We are not an exception. There are laws, principles, and processes that govern our life, but we have never been taught or shown how to understand them. They are set up to operate perfectly for each of us. If we study and understand these laws and learn how to use them, we will live harmoniously with them as *co-creators* of Life itself and achieve real freedom.

Realization
The Universe is set up perfectly for us, a support structure geared towards growth.

Laws Are Tools

The scope of the world mind is being forever expanded by modern science as we hear the word "impossible" being used less and less. Newton's third law of motion states, "To every action there is always an equal and opposite reaction." The mutual actions of any two bodies are always equal and oppositely directed. To have a single force is impossible. There must be, and always is, a pair of forces equal and opposite. Action and reaction are therefore always equal. No law of physics, chemistry, or any other science is ever free from inherent opposite or contrasted principles, the very fabric and structure of creation. The entire phenomenal world is under the essential law of polarity or duality—ebb and flow, rise and fall, day and night, pleasure and pain, birth and death—all fundamental natural activities. Electricity is a phenomenon of repulsion and attraction, its electrons and protons are electrical opposites. The atom, or final particle of matter, is like the earth itself, a magnet with positive and negative poles.

We know these laws apply to the physical plane; however, we must recognize also the existence of laws operating on subtler planes, such as the spiritual plane. All laws eventually find expression in our physical world. A "miracle" is commonly considered to be an effect without law, or beyond law. With an understanding of the subtle laws that operate in the inner consciousness, all events in our precisely adjusted universe are lawfully explicable.

As a society, we often get caught up on the surface, believing only in what we can witness with our physical senses, thinking that is all there is. Our physical senses are limited and we cannot always believe what they tell us. Modern science has already discovered that a "mystery" or "magic" of unreality pervades atomic matter. As spiritual beings living in a physical world, we must be aware of not only of physical laws, but also of spiritual laws.

Question:

How can we control and use natural laws and forces and benefit by them?

Nothing Is Lost

The most famous equation of all time is Einstein's theory of relativity, $E = mc^2$. With this theory, Einstein proved that nothing is lost in the Universe, that everything is cause and effect. If something appears to be lost, what really has happened is that it was transformed to a different level of energy. For example, when you burn wood, the wood disappears and you are left with smoke, heat, and ashes. The amount of smoke, heat, and ashes is in direct proportion to the amount of wood and the type of wood—all this is governed by specific, built-in universal laws.

Nothing is random or lost in the Universe; everything is constant in terms of cause and effect. For example, when a person eats food, the food seemingly disappears, but it actually gets transformed into human energy. As a result of eating the food, the person gains energy, which allows them to function for a specific time. The amount of energy gained is in direct proportion to the size of the individual and the size and quality of the meal, provided all abstract factors such as will power and perseverance remain constant.

If this is true, as science has proven, and nothing is lost in the Universe and all is cause and effect, then what happens when you think thoughts? And what is the result of thinking them? The effect cannot be nothing, for that is not how the Universe works! For every action —even a mere thought or emotion—provokes a corresponding reaction. INNERPOWER recognizes that thoughts are powerful forces, more subtle than electricity or magnetism, yet more powerful and potent in their essential nature. Each thought we have may eventually manifest itself on the physical plane as a fulfilled wish, dream, or goal; as a physical illness through a repeated negative thought; or as a physical healing through a repeated positive thought.

Not an End but a New Beginning

Another example is death, a very sensitive issue and a major fear for many people. However, with the understanding we now have that nothing is lost in the Universe, it is only transformed to another level of energy, what is there to fear but fear itself? Death is not an end, but a new beginning. Have you ever felt the spirit or presence of a loved one who has left the physical plane and moved on to another level? Perhaps we should compare the fear of death to the ancient fear of falling off a flat world, the fear of the unknown, or even better, the fear of what is yet to be discovered!

I have always found it interesting that everyone wants to go to Heaven, but no one wants to die. When someone does die, instead of celebrating the uplifting of a spirit to heaven, we have a memorial and wear black. Is this because we are unsure of life after death? I believe the greatest fear of many people is not dying but truly living! Perhaps the goal of the Game of Life is to create Heaven on earth.

> *Realization*
> The creative power of life makes us aware of the intimate interrelationship of all spirit and matter, and the oneness of all spirit.

Conscious Purpose Underlies Everything

For every effect in the Universe, there is a very specific cause, and it is impossible to fully understand or fix the effect without first understanding or giving consideration to the cause.

The paradox of cause and effect or creator and creation is that they are but two aspects of the same thing. The name and nature of both are always interchangeable, for one is essentially the counterpart of the other. The activity of cause is the life and form of the effect. In essence they are one, like two faces on the same coin. Can there be thought without mind, and can there be mind without thought? For one is dependent upon the other! We can at least recognize that for a thing to have being at all, it must to some extent contain the elements of the *whole*.

Question:

Can you identify the cause and effect principle operating in your life?

"I have stood on the shores of time, picking up a beautiful seashell here and there, while all before me lies the great sea of life, undiscovered."

—Sir Isaac Newton

All Is Vibration

The most powerful forces in the Universe remain unseen by us. We cannot see electricity and magnetism, yet we can certainly see their effects! In fact, our physical senses detect only a small portion of the large spectrum of sounds, colors, vibrations, and a whole lot more. Radio waves are examples of energy all around us that we cannot detect unless we have the proper instrument. Radio music is picked up on the electrical plane and is heard and felt on the material and mental planes. We know a dog's sense of smell is up to forty times greater than that of a human. If we cannot detect something, does that mean it is not there? That we are not conscious of radiation coming from something does not deny its existence. How about our sight and other limited senses? We also know through science that plants are affected by music and by the words of those who speak directly to them. Modern medicine recognizes that negative thoughts produce secretions in the body that can produce physical ailments, such as an ulcer or high blood pressure. Another example is when someone gets angry and the next thing you know they have a headache; the emotionalized thought caused the actual headache. So why do we find it so difficult to accept the idea that, if thoughts have the power to cause an illness, they also have the power to cure? We cannot see thoughts, so how do we know they exist? We experience them. With the faith and knowledge that they do exist, we can consciously use them with purpose.

The placebo effect is a perfect example; though not fully understood, it is very real. My favorite story is one a participant shared with the audience at a seminar. One afternoon at work, he had a terrible headache. He remembered that he had an aspirin in his shirt pocket. He reached into his pocket, found the aspirin, and swallowed it. Sure enough, in no time his headache went away and he was productive again. That night when he got home and took off his shirt, he noticed something in the pocket. He reached in and pulled out an aspirin. He then remembered that early that morning, his shirt button had fallen off and he had put it in the same shirt pocket as the aspirin. He had swallowed his shirt button, thinking it was an aspirin, and it had healed his headache. It is amazing what effect our mere thoughts and expectations can have!

Things Are Not as They Appear

For a long time, we believed the earth was the center of the solar system. This was quite convincing from the physical evidence—every morning the sun seemed to rise in the east and set in the west, and the stars seemed to revolve around the earth. Similarly, on the surface it seems as if life is a matter of luck, chance, or coincidence. In the sixteenth century, Copernicus hypothesized, through mathematics, that it is the sun and not the earth that is the center of the solar system. Galileo confirmed the physical truth of Copernicus' claim through the use of the telescope. Because a heliocentric claim was contrary to the literal meaning of the bible, Galileo was sentenced to house arrest for the remainder of his life. Eventually, the claim was accepted and a new belief was established. Science is constantly dropping old belief systems as new theories are discovered and proven. This is what we have to do in our life as well; we cannot be rigid in our belief systems, we must be willing and ready to drop old beliefs when they no longer serve us and adopt new ones that work. Some people are afraid to look deeper because they do not want their existing beliefs to be challenged or changed. In the course of spiritual growth, all our concepts, ideas, and beliefs have to be investigated and reevaluated over and over again. For any growth or progress to occur, we must be prepared to have many of our current belief systems expanded because they are far too limiting. So be prepared to change.

Realization
Science is always changing with new understanding.

The Earth Used to Be Flat

For a long time, humans believed the earth was flat and they lived within this limitation. Columbus in his day was thought to be an impractical dreamer, yet who has ever accomplished anything who was not a so-called dreamer? The dreams of yesterday are the realities of today!

For a long time, science believed that everything in the universe was made up of solids, liquids, and gases. In the early nineteenth century, John Dalton discovered that this belief too, was an illusion, that in fact, everything was made up of molecules. Then along came Einstein, who discovered atoms, which are even smaller than molecules. Scientists once thought that water was a single element; however, experiments later proved that two invisible elements, hydrogen and oxygen, come together in a certain combination to form water. So, from science we learn the philosophical truth that there is no material universe. Furthermore, scientists everywhere are fast approaching the same conclusion regarding the structure of all things; their underlying "material" is energy—essentially all elements are reduced to an emanating energy. All things, seen and unseen, solids, liquids, gases, energy, matter, and mind are all manifestations of different rates of vibrating energy and light. This energy is the subtle essence of all things, and the whole universe is an expression of the vitality of this consciousness. It is omnipresent, omnipotent, and omniscient.

Science has proven effective at discovering the laws of an already existing and functioning universe, yet powerless at uncovering the Sole Operator. However, science and religion can both agree to the presence of God as the intelligent, all-pervading life energy that creates all things perceptible by the senses.

"The inability of science to solve life is absolute.
This fact would be truly frightening
were it not for faith. The mystery of life is
certainly the most persistent problem ever placed
before the thought of man."
—Marconi

The Unity Underlying All of Humanity

Everything in the Universe is connected. Certainly, there could be no creation without a Creator! We cannot escape this basic fact of life. The ultimate Unity that exists is between the Universal system and ourselves, for we are an integral part of this system. As HUMANS IN TRAINING, we are related not only to each other, but also to all of nature because all life comes from one source. There is only one Creator, one Spirit called by many names, who is us all—the power, substance, and intelligence of which and through which all things are created. So when we are fighting or at war, we are committing violence against our own Self!

Because we ourselves are the cause and effect, creator and creation, we are all an indispensable part of the Universal whole. The world, the way it is now, is an outcome of all our cumulative causes and effects. Therefore, as part of the whole, the most we can do to help others is to help ourselves, and the most we can do to help ourselves is to help others! This brings the whole thing right down to the individual; the best way to promote our own interests is to promote the common interests, and the only way to preserve our own good is to preserve the good of the whole. We can no longer afford to see ourselves as separate. The Golden Rule is to "do unto others as we would have them do unto us." This rule has existed for thousands of years as part of all world religions.

The Golden Rule

African Traditional
One going to take a pointed stick to pinch a baby bird should first try it on himself to feel how it hurts.

Baha'ism
And if thine eyes be turned towards justice, choose thou for thy neighbor that which thou choosest for thyself.

Buddhism
Hurt not others in ways that you yourself would find hurtful.

Christianity
You shall love your neighbor as yourself.

Confucianism
Do not do to others what you would not like yourself.
Then there will be no resentment against you, either
in the family or in the state.

Hinduism
This is the sum of duty: do naught onto others which if
done to thee would cause thee pain.

Islamism
No one of you is a believer until he desires for his brother
that which he desires for himself.

Jainism
A man should wander about treating all creatures as he
himself would be treated.

Judaism
What is hateful to you, do not do to your fellowman.

Sikhism
As thou deemest thyself, so deem others.

Taoism
Regard your neighbor's gain as your gain, and your neighbor's loss as your own loss.

Zoroastrianism
Whatever is disagreeable to yourself do not do unto others.

*"First commit the Golden Rule to memory,
then commit it to life."*

—Edwin Markham

Self-Fulfilling

The force that designed and created the Universe cannot be considered an unintelligent or blind force moving with no conscious direction. Instead, it is an intelligent force that knows exactly what it is doing. It has created an intelligent Universe and it is now moving towards an intelligent purpose. This all-pervading, creative energy emanating from all of life is aware of itself, aware of what it is doing, and aware of how to do it. Because of this, anyone who works with the intelligence of that force can accomplish all things through it! So we must recognize that all creative force of the Universe must be subjected to the direction of intelligence. Electricity, for example, to be used in our everyday life, must be governed by intelligence, or else we would not have light, heat, and power. Electricity by itself is a blind force, yet when subjected to the control of intelligence, it produces constructive results. When used properly, it becomes our servant, and when handled ignorantly, it is a deadly force. INNERPOWER is like electricity in the sense that both must have a nonresistant instrument to channel their power.

Question:

With the knowledge that God is absolute, omnipresent, omnipotent, and omniscient, where can Heaven or hell exist except in our consciousness?

We Create Our Own World

Our life is a reflection of who we are inside. Within each of us is the cause of every experience, good or bad, that has ever happened to us. No disease, accident, or even natural disaster of any kind can ever happen to us without our first causing it on some individual or global level. Imagine dropping a pebble into a bowl of water—this exactly represents every thought or word we think or speak. The thought or word sets in motion certain vibrations that go out in ever-widening circles, eventually returning to the center. Every thought or word we think or speak, be it good or bad, returns to us as certainly as we send it forth. Who and what we are right now is an accumulation and combination of all the thoughts, feelings, words, and actions that we have created up until this very moment. Our thoughts, feelings, words, and actions are all energy that radiates like a radio signal. This energy vibrates at a certain level. The level at which this energy vibrates individualizes us. The vibration of our energy attracts people, things, or circumstances into our life. This explains why sometimes people keep attracting the same type of person or experience over and over again—their vibration does not change because the lesson has not yet been learned. Our particular vibration also explains why some people are consistently "lucky" and others never seem to get a break. As we change from the inside, our personal vibration will change and our personal reality will match our newly changed personal vibration. When we lay the blame on "good breaks" or "bad breaks"—there is that "luck" again!—we have yet to take full responsibility. Our life has everything to do with us!

Are you sensitive to the energy of the people and places around you? This energy can be positive or negative, strengthening or weakening, and perhaps it is why we like or do not like to be around certain individuals or in certain environments.

*"The Universe works with you and for you,
it is not your enemy."*
—David Spangler

Consciousness-Raising for Success

We can progress in life as far as our individual consciousness progresses. The idea is to get away from the formed opinions and judgments of others that have led to a sense of separation and to bring ourselves into the consciousness of our Oneness with the Universal whole.

We experience ourselves as separate from everything else, and this sense of separation makes us feel insecure and afraid. The creative power of life makes us aware of the intimate interrelationship of all spirit and matter, and the Oneness of all spirit. Consciousness is where the separation begins, and we see the effects in the physical world. In human consciousness, complications seem to develop because the ego interferes with the Soul's sincere desire to learn and move forward. Life and consciousness are inseparable. Life is the outward manifestation of consciousness. Before we can realize our INNERPOWER, we must first expand our awareness and deepen our understanding to see life as it really is—consciousness itself.

Understanding the role of consciousness in all life enables us to see that life is indeed a process of inward force—consciousness—working itself out into outward form, from the seed that becomes a flower to the thoughts that become our reality. There is nothing in the physical world that did not begin in the invisible! When we reach this level of understanding, we can begin to participate more fully in the process of life and enjoy its journey.

Realization
The more we know, the more we are responsible for.

Intentional Awareness

It is all a matter of awareness—all levels of understanding

originate from it. Consciousness is our state of awareness, our sensitivity to the energy around us, and our capacity to know and understand our world and ourselves. Consciousness is determined by the concepts or beliefs that we hold in our mind, and it alone determines our success, happiness, and quality of life. As we expand our consciousness, a new level of understanding comes about and through this we can erase old limitations and give up old estimates of ourselves while accepting new possibilities.

> ## Realization
> The way that the world works is based on consciousness. Each of us is blessed with this gift, yet how many choose to consciously exercise it?

To achieve the quality of life we want, we must come to the understanding that for positive changes to last in the long term, those changes must occur at the deepest level. Consciousness is the deepest level, the cause and creator of the behaviors and habits that control our life. To change our behavior without first changing our consciousness is an exercise in futility, not to mention frustration. Insanity has been defined as "doing the same thing over and over and expecting a different result." As we develop and raise our consciousness, our behavior and habits will naturally adjust to the changes within.

LIFE SKILL
Expand awareness and identify, not with a limited body, but with the Universal structure.

From Surviving to Thriving

We can benefit so much from the wisdom of great souls. Their thoughts are there to help us expand and improve our mind. There are so many inspiring things worth knowing and discovering, yet so many people spend their time foolishly in search of distraction and quick fixes.

When there is a lack of satisfaction internally, we turn to the outer world for distraction to mask our Soul's hunger. As a society, we have become masters of distraction with so many possibilities: television, diets, alcohol, drugs, fast food—with all these distractions dominating our life, we easily forget what is beneath the surface and think these fleeting pleasures are the aim of life. Then, when we face setbacks and disappointments, we wonder what went wrong.

What is necessary to experience true love and happiness is an understanding of the deeper needs that all HUMANS IN TRAINING have in common. These cannot be found in the temporary world without, only in the unchangeable world within. Acquiring knowledge of the world outside can help us to tap into our INNERPOWER, the source of true love and happiness. Knowledge of the world is not simply about information of the physical world; it is also information that enables us to gain insight into our inner functioning, because the outer world is only a reflection of the inner.

It is impossible for anyone to find peace, happiness, and success as long as they are expecting anyone or anything to do for them what they alone can and must do for themselves. We already have the power within. No one can give us what we already have and awaken in us what we ourselves refuse to express. As long as we expect the world and other people to fix our problems, we will only meet with disappointment.

> *Realization*
> The awakened individual understands their work is forever with themselves.

Too often we complain about what we do not have. As soon as we do that, we are not making the most out of what we do have. If we made the most of what we have, it would certainly bring us more of what we want. When we get too involved in the things over which we have no control, we adversely affect the things over which we do have control. If we focus on what we cannot do, we hardly notice or do what we can.

LIFE SKILL
Do not make excuses for your flaws.

The Very Essence of Life

Failure to take the time or make the effort to better understand our world and ourselves is the number-one reason for unhappiness. By developing a deeper understanding, we will discover beyond all possible doubt that *Love* creates and sustains the Universe, and that all of us are destined to discover this *Love*—the very essence of life. We all belong to the same Creator; we all have the same Life Force working behind us to keep us alive physically. We all search for meaning, happiness, and purpose of life, and we all want to love and be loved.

All the World Is Home

We are all waves in the great ocean of Spirit. Recognize that it is the force of the ocean behind the wave that gives the wave its power! Each wave comes and returns to the ocean and each wave is the same, yet at the same time unlike any other, and most importantly, each wave *is* the ocean. That same power exists within each of us. It is our responsibility to know that we are the ocean and to develop this power if we are to know the measure of our own Soul.

> *"It's not how much we do, but how much love we put into doing.*
> *It's not how much we give, but how much love we put into giving.*
> *To God there is nothing small.*
> *The moment we have given to God, it becomes infinite."*
> —Mother Theresa

Our Deepest Fear

"Our deepest fear is not that we are inadequate. Our deepest fear is that we are powerful beyond measure. It is our light, not our darkness, that most frightens us.

We ask ourselves, who am I to be brilliant, gorgeous, talented and fabulous? Actually, who are you not be be?

You are a child of God. Your playing small does not serve the world. There is nothing enlightened about shrinking so that other people won't feel insecure about you. We were born to manifest the glory of God that is within us.

It's not just in some of us; it's in everyone.

And as we let our own light shine, we unconsciously give other people permission to do the same. As we are liberated from our own fear, our presence automatically liberates other."

~From **A Return To Love** *by Marianne Williamson~*

A Perfect World

- All forces are governed by intelligence.
- The Universe is set up perfectly for us, a support structure geared towards growth.
- Nothing can truly be considered a miracle except in the profound sense that everything is a miracle!
- INNERPOWER is achieved through knowledge of spiritual law.
- Thoughts are living things.
- Thoughts and words are a tremendous vibratory force, shaping our body and our life.
- Science is always changing with new understanding.
- The intelligence in all creation is a reflection of the intelligence beyond all creation.
- The more we know, the more we are responsible for.
- The awakened individual understands their work is forever with themselves.

*"The day children realize all adults
are not perfect they become adolescents.
The day they forgive them they become adults.
The day they forgive themselves
they find compassion."*

—Alden Nolan

CHAPTER SIX

Humans In Training

Life is a process of self-discovery—rediscovering who we are, why we are here, our value, and the value of all human beings as Citizens of the World!

Remembering Where We Came From!

To know oneself is the simplest yet hardest thing in life. It is the key that opens the door to our creative and spiritual potential so we can experience true love, health, abundance, and perfect self-expression. It is the solution that can end all of humankind's sufferings, sorrows, and miseries. Self-knowledge is supreme knowledge. Men and women of great wisdom and light have handed down this knowledge to us throughout the ages. They have informed us of this ideal way by word and by the example they themselves have set. These wise men and women have wanted us to learn and understand the value and importance of knowing *who we really are*, and what it means to be an enlightened, empowered human being— the highest and most select channel through which life manifests itself.

*R*ealization
Gain self-knowledge for the purpose of gaining inner freedom.

These teachings have been given to us because we have become disoriented in our knowledge of who we really are. Yes, we know our name, address, important numbers, where we work, our hopes and dreams, what we like and dislike, and even our secret failings. But the wise teachers meant that we should come to know our depth, our capacity and potential, and what role we are here to play. The teachings of these great ones serve as guidelines, which, if followed faithfully and devotedly, will enlighten our consciousness to the realization of our true spiritual identity.

One of the great philosophers said, "Despite everything else, a wise man should strive after knowledge of Self, for there is no knowledge that is higher, or that brings more satisfaction of power, than a knowledge of his own being." So, my dearest friends and fellow teammates, let us strive determinedly together and never give up until we gain full knowledge of our whole being!

Realization
Change yourself and you have done your part in changing the world.

When we truly know who we really are, we will discover that we are very powerful, much more than we have ever imagined or been taught—although perhaps we have been taught—yet we just never fully comprehended because the scope of our mind is far too limited. We are destined to know how to gain access to the unlimited gifts and treasures that are our birthright. We will also discover and be able to tap into all our inherent abilities. We were able to do so as children; however, as adults, we have lost this ability. As long as we lack self-knowledge, we do not really know these things. Why? Because we have a mind whose scope and potential has hardly been tapped, and a Soul whose limits we have yet to test. In essence, it is a re-definition of identity.

> ### Realization
> You are your very own masterpiece; you get to create whatever you want!

Question:
Although we do not always get out of life what we want, we get out of life who we are. Who are you?

We Are Multi-Dimensional in Nature

It is evident that, as humans, we have no real understanding of ourselves or of our importance as part of the Universe. Our life revolves too much around physical matter; we often forget that we are a multi-dimensional being with not only a body, but also a mind and spirit to manage and take care of. We have a responsibility to the body—to keep it fit; a responsibility to the mind—to develop its powers; and a responsibility to the Soul—to pray and meditate daily. As spiritual beings, if we neglect the Soul, eventually our body and mind will also suffer!

Realization
In order to heal the body, we must first heal the Soul.

We tend to think of ourselves as separate individuals, when in fact we are all interconnected on an energetic level. Just as something that affects one part of the body can spread and affect the entire body, so can something that affects one person, community, or country, spread and affect everyone and everything else, from the microscopic level of the atom to the macroscopic level of the Universe. As a result of our ignorance of our true nature, we experience from the depth of our heart, consciously or subconsciously, a homesickness—a longing to go home, yet we are uncertain as to where this home may be. This emptiness can never be filled with anything less than an experience of our true Self. For many people, their mind races faster than life, in constant search of people or things that they think would make them happy. This could be money, winning an award, recognition, a job promotion, a brand new car, a bigger house, or a better lover. Unfortunately, however, this is a confusing and bitter search because we can never depend on something that lies outside of ourselves to provide lasting happiness. Those who believe that happiness lies in the fulfillment of their desires will find that happiness is always just around the corner, a corner that rarely gets turned. We do not need anything outside of ourselves to make us happy so much as we need divine knowledge of our true nature, so that we can apply it to the inner work that will liberate us from our own self-ignorance.

> ## *Realization*
> Life is all a matter of individual spiritual evolution.

Learning to Listen

Inner work involves searching *within* for the meaning and purpose of our life and being. The answers are always inside us. To be able to listen and to receive them, we have to take the time to be absolutely still and go deep within and not be hypnotized by a whirlpool of mental and emotional confusion that never seems to stop. Getting to know ourselves on a deeper level can be compared to trying to remember something we have forgotten, because everything we have ever wanted to know about ourselves is already within us—all we have to do is "remember" it.

As we come to know the greater stranger—ourselves—we discover our most dangerous enemy, our truest friend, our wisest teacher, and our safest advisor, all rolled into one. To know ourselves as we *actually* are, rather than our interpretation of who we are—or, perhaps more accurately, misinterpretation— means giving up old ideas of who we *think* we are while accepting new possibilities. We are both the problem and the solution; this is good news, as it implies that we, and no one else, control our progress. We, and no one else, choose to make our life meaningful by learning about and developing ourselves. So how do we get to this point? The quickest and most powerful method of personal, professional, and spiritual development is Self-knowledge.

> *Realization*
> To live and not to know one's Self is to live without identity.

Humility through Self-Understanding

Humility is an experience of the Oneness of humanity and an understanding of all that we have in common. It leads to a balanced outlook on human nature that is accepting of all our strengths and weaknesses. The act of attributing certain powers to others and denying them for ourselves is what keeps us from experiencing our own INNERPOWER. To be truly humble requires taking an honest look at ourselves and coming to clearly know our abilities and weaknesses. When you develop Self-knowledge, you will realize that no one is above or below you—that you are the equal of any person. The same power is alive within each of us, yet it often remains dormant. It is our business to develop our full capacity if we are to know the measure of our own Soul. So let us be bold in accepting as our birthright that whatever the great ones have accomplished and proven in their lives, we can accomplish as well. This is what they taught. It is a great privilege to know that we all possess equal potential, and it is our responsibility to develop it if we want to experience what they taught. What purpose does it serve if we "gain the whole world and lose our Soul"?

To be the best we can, we need to know who we are and why we think, feel, and act the way we do. As we begin to understand how we function naturally, we can then proceed to make a conscious effort to work in harmony with ourselves. Then, and only then, will we witness significant progress on all levels and in all areas of our life. When our personal evolution is honest, we can respect who we are, and this deep acceptance of our nature leads to a wider understanding and greater respect for others. We are also motivated to help others with their problems and support them in cultivating their capabilities. We also see that we all share similar goals of happiness and fulfillment, and we are subject to similar problems and difficulties.

> ### Realization
> Life is a mirror, we see ourselves in our teammates.

The Gift of Self-Respect

It is very difficult to fully appreciate and believe in something you do not understand, and it is even more difficult to respect something you do not believe in. If you do not believe in yourself, you will not dare to dream or even try to do very much with your life, and all your gifts and talents will remain dormant and undeveloped. As you develop greater self-awareness and a deeper self-understanding, you begin to believe in yourself because now you are starting to know yourself as you *actually* are, and not as you *think* you are. Along with believing in yourself comes greater self-respect. Suddenly it no longer seems so difficult, or such a chore, to take better care of yourself. We do not usually take care of the things we do not respect; most people have only to look in the mirror, at our environment, and at how we treat each other to confirm that! I have always been amazed at what people will do for a complete stranger that they would not do for themselves!

LIFE SKILL
Protect yourself and be discriminating in what you expose yourself to mentally, emotionally, physically, and spiritually.

As we get to know and appreciate the miracle of the body, mind, and spirit, we feel it is both a privilege and an honor not only to have them, but also to take care of them. When we have this appreciation, we become very selective about what we allow to come into the feedback mechanism of our body, mind, and spirit—not only from the world outside ourselves, but also from our own thoughts, feelings, words, and actions. We can choose to let in only positive, uplifting energy such as love, joy, or optimism, and avoid or protect ourselves from negative, down-pulling energy such as hatred, depression, judgment, or pessimism. As we exercise discrimination, we begin to feel a greater sense of connection with everyone and everything around us, including our source and ourselves. We know that it is quite common for that connection to get a little fuzzy every once in a while, especially when we are wrapped up with our own and our world's problems. We must learn to create within ourselves a kingdom of happiness, a fortress of unshakable peace and security, and a temple of divine communion.

We must improve our knowing! We must study ourselves—the difference between the state of our minds and the state of our Souls, and where we are and where we are meant to be.

> *Realization*
> The process of enlightenment is the path of learning to appreciate the Light within those we love and within ourselves.

"With all thy getting, get understanding."
—Proverb

Learning to Love

Getting along with ourselves is the most important part of getting along with everyone and everything else in this world. It is difficult to truly love anyone or anything if you do not love yourself. To those who do not love themselves, yet *think* they love someone else, I suggest that their love is not true love; it is pure attachment, which is the manifestation of love in its lower form. Paradoxically, until you love everyone and everything else in creation, you cannot say that you truly love yourself. If you think you love yourself, and yet there is any part of creation you do not love, then your love is not pure. When we truly love someone, we love the Light within that person. Such is life—all is interconnected.

Question:

Do you see the same Light and energy in all people and in all creations?

> **Realization**
> We do not injure enemies through hating them; we hurt only ourselves.

Where there is Love, there is expansion. The opposite energy—contraction—manifests as criticism, judgment, or hatred. If we begin hating and judging someone because they do not fulfill our expectations or do what we want, we end up contracting our personality and isolating ourselves. Criticizing, hating, and being angry all deplete energy. Are you constantly fighting with yourself in your mind? If people cannot get along with themselves, how can they expect to get along with others? First and foremost we need to learn to appreciate and love ourselves. Face it, you cannot escape from you! You are your lifetime guarantee! You carry your body, mind, and spirit with you no matter where you go, so learn to love yourself while at the same time learning to love everyone and everything around you; be aware that the same life energy flows through all of creation.

LIFE SKILL
To know beyond all possible doubt that love creates and sustains the Universe, and that all God's creations are destined to discover this love.

Identify the Killers of Spirit

I once asked a group of senior students what they thought were the two biggest killers in our society. Their answers were quick and predictable: heart disease, cancer, and AIDS. However, I was there to talk to them about two other killers, ones that kill more dreams and spirits than anything else—self-doubt and fear of failure. These are attitudes we take on when we lack faith and trust not only in ourselves, but also in the Universe to do its part to guide and help us. Self-doubt and fear of failure have never accomplished anything positive or constructive and never will. They do nothing but stunt our growth and progress, paralyze us, and prevent us from being an active player in the Game of Life. They are just a figment of imagination and have no substantial truth in and of themselves. May we learn to see through their fictitious nature so that we can understand that they are not real and have no power over us *unless* we give them the authority. When we break free from the illusions of doubts and fears, we can achieve anything in life.

> ## Realization
> A lack of true identity is reflected in an individual's insecurities.

To actively participate in the evolution of consciousness, we must let go of our doubts and fears. They are just an illusion, created in our minds. An illusion is not real. It has no power in and of itself. Because we know that doubts and fears are just an illusion, we can no longer excuse ourselves from taking responsibility for our life and living on all levels—with our whole being.

> ## Realization
> The will to "do" springs from the understanding that we "can do"!

Track Down the Killers

One powerful method for helping us to see through the nature of doubts and fears and finally eliminate them from our life is self-analysis. Many people never analyze themselves. Mentally, they are mechanical products of the factory of their environment. They preoccupy themselves mainly with working, eating, sleeping, and going here and there to be entertained. They do not know why they do this, or what it is they are seeking. They think they know, yet as soon as they find what they were looking for, they feel that the satisfaction is only temporary, and so they start to seek after something else, and thus the circle of seeking repeats itself like a cat chasing its own tail. True happiness keeps eluding them and they wonder why. Those who avoid self-analysis can never fully experience life. Instead, their life is interpreted as a series of random or accidental events, and they live as if they were robots, conditioned by their environment and habits.

Unless you analyze yourself and find out why you are the way you are, or why you do the things you do, you will always remain more or less the same person, with no significant change or progress. True self-analysis is the greatest means of progress along our spiritual journey, so learn to practice it for your own benefit. Do not wait until life gives you no alternative but to change. Get into the habit of examining yourself by reflecting on these questions: Who am I? Where did I come from, and where am I going? What do I really want in my life? What area of my life do I have to pay more attention to? How can I improve myself? What is preventing me from being happy, and how can I fix that? Reflect and contemplate these questions and answer them honestly. The first two questions may require you to do some research because they require *absolute* answers. As you reflect, write down all your answers and ideas in a journal and start to apply them in your daily life. The end of the day is a great time for self-analysis, think of it as a part of your cool-down time.

It is difficult for many people to change, mainly because they do not want to see, or admit to, their own faults. In order to expand our awareness, we need to learn to open our hearts and minds and be receptive to the feedback and information that is both within us and all around us. Let's make self-reflection an integral part of our everyday living and not wait until disaster strikes. Let's not wait until something is broken to fix it!

LIFE SKILL
Keep a mental diary. Spend a few introspective minutes every day asking yourself questions such as: How did I behave today? How did I respond to others?

So analyze, analyze, and analyze! Introspection is the mirror of your Soul. Take time for introspection every day and be aware of where you need to improve or change, and then do it. Remember to write down everything. As you go within, you will discover more about who and what you are, rather than who and what you imagine yourself to be, and this will automatically lead to the eradication of doubts and fears from your life.

A Turn of the Page

Meeting my biological mother was a real gift and privilege, and I am extremely grateful for it. However, I still felt frustrated inside. Thinking I needed a change in my life, I took a vacation. I traveled to Europe for two months to explore other cultures, hoping deep down to find answers. I had a great time and met some wonderful people; however, I also discovered that, across all cultures and countries, everyone has the same needs and questions!

Making Another Connection

When I returned from my journey, I paid my biological mother a visit. She showed me a beautiful album of letters and pictures of our reunion. One topic we had not spent a lot of time on was my biological father. She revealed very little about their relationship. I did know, however, that he had gone on to be a highly successful businessman. Unfortunately, the year before I met her, he had died in a high-speed car accident!

While I was going through the album, my mother left the room for a moment. Something made me turn directly to the back of the album where I found a scrunched-up piece of newspaper. I opened it up and, to my surprise, it was a front-page story featuring my father's car accident. I saw a picture of him for the first time. I quickly read the article and discovered that I had a half-brother and a half-sister and that my father had owned a company in partnership with his brother. When I finished reading the article, I carefully placed the paper back into the album and did not say anything to my mother because I was unsure about how sensitive the subject might be.

Making a Different Kind of Connection

On my way home, I had to drive through the city where my biological father had lived. From my car, I called the operator to get the phone number of the family business. I then called the company to get directions and to find out whether my uncle was there. Shortly after, I arrived at the office building and talked my way into seeing my uncle, the president. I walked into his office, closing the door behind me. My uncle was on the phone, but he quickly hung up. I introduced myself and told him I was there to speak about his brother. I asked him straight out if he knew whether his brother had had another child. He stood up from his desk and came towards me with his arms wide open and gave me a hug that I will never forget. He told me that when I walked through the door, he felt that he was looking at his own brother, who had been his best friend. He also shared with me that he and his brother often talked about me, and that he had wanted to meet me more than anything else in the world. My uncle canceled his lunch so we could talk; it was like seeing an old friend I had not spoken to for years. It was an amazing day of discovery for both of us. Lunch turned into dinner, and we talked late into the night. We spent almost every day together for the next few weeks, catching up on all the missing years, playing golf, and doing a whole lot more. One of the most special times of my life was the evening that I spent with my uncle and my biological mother. It was magical listening to them answer each other's questions that had been unanswered for years.

Surrendering to Your Purpose

The one day that we did not spend together, my uncle died in a high-speed car accident in almost the same way my biological father had died. I was grateful for the three incredible weeks that we had spent together; however, now I was even more confused. My soul-searching was entering a deeper level. I felt I had no choice but to surrender. I always had a sense of how precious life is, but now, with an even greater sense of life's value, I felt an urgency to get it "on purpose." I prayed and prayed, asking God what His will was for me. I reflected on my life, my uniqueness, my gifts, and my passions. I asked myself "What has life been preparing me for?" The answer to this question had been staring me in the face all along, yet I had never seen it, or perhaps I had but was too afraid to see it. I might have tricked myself, both unconsciously and consciously, into thinking that I did not know the answer. However, now was not the time to play tricks on myself because by doing so, I would only be cheating my teammates and myself. Now was the time to take action. I could no longer go on with this kind of frustration; many changes were needed inside and out.

> *Realization*
> If you really want to make a difference, find the courage and commitment to understand yourself and live your life on purpose!

The Rewards of Being Unique

You are far more unique than you might think, far beyond your physical appearance. Your life experiences and the interpretations that you give them are unique. No one can live your life for you. It is the uniqueness of our life's journey that gives every one of us an opportunity to contribute to life's infinite diversity. Therefore, no one should feel that they have nothing to contribute. What are you contributing? Your contribution towards life—no matter how big or small—is required, in its rightful place, to make up the perfect whole in the vast scheme of life.

We live in a society that rewards people financially and in other ways, such as with fame and recognition, for what they do that is special. We measure our value according to how easy or difficult we are to replace. However, if we are true to ourselves, and therefore to our uniqueness, we will discover that we have no competition. No one can be a better you than you yourself! As long as you try to be someone else, you will never know who you really are and the best of you will be ignored. Recognize what we have in common while you're working on your own unique gifts and abilities, but remember that it is our uniqueness that makes us special. Why would you want to accept second best, when the best in you is waiting to be accepted by you?

> *Realization*
> Your Purpose is your Service and Contribution to the world!

Know Thy Product

I love to challenge people to discover their uniqueness. At a seminar for financial consultants, I asked the group what they were selling. They responded that they sold mutual funds and other financial products, so I asked them again. When I still didn't get the answer I was looking for, I told them, "What you are selling is yourself. If the customer does not buy you, nothing else matters." I asked one consultant, Phil, "You are the product, you are what people are buying, so what makes you unique?" He responded that he was honest. I asked if anyone else in the room was honest, and they all said they were. Phil further added that he had his clients' best interest at heart, and again everyone else said they did as well. So I asked Phil if he would do business with himself and why.

As you can see, it is very difficult to share or sell something you do not know or understand, and even more difficult if you are selling the wrong thing. As a HUMAN IN TRAINING, you must know all about you—your gifts and talents, strengths and weaknesses, and what makes you unique—because you are the product. If you do not know your product, how can you expect others to want it?

> ## Realization
> Everything in creation has individuality. Appreciate your uniqueness and build on it; it is what others are drawn to and, more importantly, it is yours to share!

We discover our uniqueness by examining those activities that we are naturally drawn towards and love doing—activities that energize us rather than take our energy away. Once we discover our uniqueness and express it in our daily life, we become a channel for creative energy from the Universe to flow and work through us. We begin to love what we do and who we are. This happens to us when we employ our unique abilities in our work, and it is greatly satisfying when we are paid for what we most love to do. Only when we allow ourselves to express our unique ability in daily life will we feel a deep sense of purpose and fulfillment. Life itself becomes simple, loving, and joyful. Life has been preparing you to do just that! So open your mind and your heart. You can experience Heaven right here on earth, and you can find it in the work we are all here to do! Simply look within to discover your own unique ability, everyone has it! And when you have found it, have the *courage* to express it in daily life. Do not be afraid to take the first steps required to exercise your unique abilities, no matter how faltering at first. Have absolute faith and trust that the Universe will always guide you and be with you all the way.

Question:

What is your unique gift and contribution to society?

Realization A gift is something that is meant to be given away.

You may think that the world
does not need you,
But it does.
For you are unique,
unlike anyone who has ever been before
or will come again.
No one can say your piece,
speak your voice,
smile your smile, or shine
your light.
Who knows how many travelers will lose
their way
as they try to pass by your
empty place in the
darkness.

~Anonymous~

*"Live according to your highest light
and more light shall be given."*
—Peace Pilgrim

*R*ealization
**Put to work for constructive purposes
the power you already have and more
will come!**

Clear Communication Is Key!

Let's consider a well-known study completed at UCLA that is referred to in many seminars dealing with effective communication. Results indicate that effective communication is 55 percent physiology, 38 percent tonality, and only 7 percent vocabulary.

Physiology, according to this study, plays a major role in effective communication because first impressions are important and our posture and facial expressions can reveal a lot about ourselves. Of tonality, the sound of one word can leave many different impressions, which can affect the clarity and understanding of what you are communicating. You've probably experienced this many times in your personal and professional relationships. Of vocabulary, the same word can have many different interpretations and definitions. Have you ever witnessed people arguing when they all think they are right, according to their own definitions and interpretations? Success means different things to different people; for everyone to be on the same wavelength, it is important to establish common definitions.

If the conclusions of this UCLA study were correct, why was it that when I was listening to a speaker who had great physiology, was well dressed, had great tonality as a professionally trained speaker, and had an excellent vocabulary, I still had one major problem? I did not believe a word this person was saying. According to the study, this speaker was an effective communicator. I believe the qualities that were missing were *authenticity* and *genuineness*, two critical factors that cannot be bought or faked. These intangible factors, in my opinion, play a greater role in determining the effectiveness of a presentation. People know intuitively whether someone is speaking from their head or from their heart. Gandhi, for example, did not have great posture or tonality, yet he had something greater, a deep passion, a commitment, and a Soul purpose that could only come from deep within. We all know the great influence he had on millions of people. When we combine the intangible and the tangible factors of effective communication with a deep passion for the topic, we become a truly effective communicator.

Realization
Effective communication begins within.

> *"My life is my teaching."*
> —Gandhi

Getting Out of the Sandbox

As we adopt a new philosophy for ourselves and start to consciously live by it, we begin to form a new sense of identity. I believe a strong identity is what many people are missing in their life. Along with a strong identity comes a belief in oneself that is absolutely required to build unshakable self-confidence, which is much needed if we want to succeed in today's world.

Your self-image is not a mirror of who you really are; it is what determines who and what you are at the moment, or will become in the future. Your self-image is often a misconception of who you really are, and you will always be consistent with who and what you *think* you are. Most people think their self-image accurately reflects who and what they really are. In reality, however, it is a creation that we have developed rather haphazardly over the years as a result of impressions and feedback from countless people, circumstances, and misinterpretations. Your self-image can be the biggest box or prison you have ever put yourself into because through your personal beliefs you can convince yourself that you are something you are not, and consequently you never expand beyond your personal self-image.

Most of what we have been taught or have accepted about ourselves is either limiting or totally wrong. An example is a story a friend once told me about the time in his childhood when he arrived three weeks late for kindergarten. For three weeks, the class had been practicing painting trees. On his first day, he thought he painted a pretty nice tree. When he looked at the other kids' paintings, however, he decided that his was not as good, so he came to the conclusion that he was a lousy painter. When the teacher asked him if he would rather play in the sandbox or paint, what do you think he chose? For the next fifty years, he still did not try painting because no one had explained to him that the other kids had just had more practice. We should all learn from this teammate and never let ourselves be caught in the sandbox of our own misinterpreted or restricted self-image.

IDENTITY versus CONFIDENCE

It would be a pretty boring world if we all agreed with each other all the time—certainly we would not learn very much, or very quickly. In addition, agreeing about something can be very dangerous without first examining its truthfulness and validity. The holocaust of World War II is an example of what can happen when a group of people all agree with one individual's belief without first examining its truthfulness and validity. The result was disastrous and cost millions of lives. When we have a strong awareness of our identity, we do not allow the interpretations or beliefs of others to affect our confidence, values, and standards. We know who we are, and no matter what others tell us, good or bad, we do not accept what they say without question. We stand strong in our beliefs, values, and standards, yet at the same time, we open our minds and hearts with discrimination to the feedback and messages in our environment.

I remember the first time that, as an athlete, I had my confidence stripped away and I felt intimidated. This sounds funny to me now that I know that no one can actually do such a thing to another. But at the time, it really disturbed me. A series of events, both on and off the ice, made me question who I was. I also began to question my abilities as an athlete. I obviously did not believe that I was as good as other people had been telling me I was, because the first time this idea was challenged, I began to question myself. It was then that I decided that confidence alone was not good enough and that to perform to my potential, I must build myself an identity, one that could not be shaken or challenged by anyone because I, and no one else, created it. Because I created my own identity, no one can know me as I do. Other people are entitled to their opinion, whether right or wrong or whether or not I agree with them; however, the only opinion that really matters is mine! Whether given a compliment or criticism, I now accept it as an opinion and extract from it what I can to make myself a better person. Once we are ready to accept full responsibility for our life, we begin by consciously building and creating a strong identity through the power of reconditioning our consciousness.

LIFE SKILL
The ability to extract the highest and best from each person and experience, and not to take everything personally

World Peace through Inner Peace

At the root of all our environmental problems, such as pollution and piles of garbage, are our own inner pollution and garbage. The outer is a reflection of the inner—where we are as a whole. The state of our world today gives us a huge clue as to how much house-cleaning we need to do internally. War is an example of the battle going on inside the hearts and minds of humankind. To have peace and love in the world, we must first have peace and love within ourselves.

> ## Realization
> The way we can contribute most effectively to world peace is to live in peace within ourselves.

Question:

How much are we carrying around inside ourselves that we should have let go of long ago? How many scars, regrets, missed opportunities, mistakes? How long are we willing to carry them?

Power of Forgiveness

To see others and ourselves as HUMANS IN TRAINING is the practice of giving others—parents, family, friends, coworkers, and even strangers—the benefit of the doubt. They are doing the best they can at their current level; they are in training just like you and I. Give them and yourself the freedom to explore and experience life without interference or judgment. Choose to learn from each other's strengths and weaknesses rather than blaming others or living in the past, unable to move beyond. Take responsibility for all aspects of your life and accept whatever comes your way as a consequence of your decisions or indecision, actions or inaction. Know that nothing can ever happen to you without your having brought the very experience into your life through thought, feeling, word, or deed. Often what happens to you is a reaction to what is going on in your mind. Therefore, you must be very careful of what you are creating inside your head. If you are creating loving thoughts, you attract loving people. If you are creating greedy thoughts, you attract greedy people—we all know that "like attracts like." Nevertheless, if you think someone has done you wrong, forgive them and move on. This benefits everyone and removes any excuse by either party for not moving on with their life. It is far better to love your enemies and pray for them; you are doing a double service, to yourself and to them. Realize that only to the extent that you can forgive others, can you forgive yourself. Essentially, however, there is no one to forgive because the real you can never be hurt by anyone or anything; it is only your ego that is hurt and needs to learn forgiveness.

Realization
Unforgivingness is the most prolific cause of dis-ease.

LIFE SKILL
Learn to forgive, heal, and love yourself and others.

The Story of the Two Monks

Once upon a time many moons ago, two monks were walking in silence through the forest—a younger monk, Anjan, and an older monk, Nanda.

Eventually their path led to a stream. There they saw a beautiful young lady, exquisitely clad, standing on the bank. She was in great distress because she wanted to cross the stream but did not know how without getting her fine, long robes wet.

Without hesitation, Nanda scooped her up, crossed the stream, and set her down on dry ground. She thanked him and continued on her way and the monks continued on theirs, again in silence.

Anjan was uncertain, distressed, and confused. He became more and more restless and then finally he spoke.

"Brother Nanda," he said. "I do not know what to make of it. You know our order is an austere order, and we cannot so much as speak to a woman. But… but… you saw that lady, you…uh… picked her up and… carried her across the stream! And yet…" he continued, almost choking, "You just keep on walking as if nothing happened!"

"It is quite simple," Nanda replied. "I set her down on the opposite bank, but you, Brother Anjan, are still carrying her!"

So… who, indeed, had the lighter burden, and the lighter step?

Buddhist Tale

Humans In Training

- Change yourself and you have done your part in changing the world.
- Life is all a matter of individual spiritual evolution.
- Life is a mirror, we see ourselves in our teammates.
- We do not injure enemies by hating them; we hurt only ourselves.
- A lack of true identity is reflected in an individual's insecurities.
- Your Purpose is your Service and Contribution to the world!
- A gift is something that is meant to be given away.
- Effective communication begins within.
- We can contribute most effectively to world peace by living in peace within ourselves.
- Unforgivingness is the most prolific cause of dis-ease.

"*History is a vast early warning system.*"
—Norman Cousins

CHAPTER SEVEN

A World in Transition

Entering the Age of Consciousness—Despite ever-changing world conditions, in the larger picture, life has a profound purpose; we are on a universal journey that will ultimately reveal who we are and why we are here!

It Is a New World We Face, and We Must Mold Ourselves to the Changes!

As our understanding of our world and how it works increases, we come to realize that, in a constantly expanding universe, change is inherent in all things. It is a constant factor in the Universe. Are we not now in the most transformational time in human history? Change is occurring at a faster rate now than ever. This can be both scary and exciting. So, are we prepared?

Today, technology is probably the single most important influence in our world. It is radically redefining our society: how we travel, communicate, do business, and most importantly, how we see ourselves. This new age demands that we constantly set new standards, new visions, and renew integrity. Today's problems can only be solved through deep understanding and individual spiritual growth. The inner spiritual transformation of people, through each individual's moral and spiritual effort, is the only way to change this world. When we make the effort to change ourselves spiritually, we help not only ourselves, but also our families and all those with whom we come in contact. The time is now; feel the urgency! Only through our spiritual maturity and a strong inner foundation will we come together as both a family and a team to solve world conditions. If we continue as we are, we will surely destroy ourselves and the planet that sustains us.

> **Realization**
> The inner spiritual transformation of individuals is the only way to change this world.

The Law of Change

We cannot escape the Law of Change. We live in a world with few guarantees; however, the nature of matter is change—constant motion. It is important to understand that everything in the Universe is in the process of changing and becoming something else—from subatomic particles, the weather, and the seasons, to the sun and beyond. Our body continuously changes; from birth to death, it goes through constant degeneration and renewal. Our careers and finances change. Our relationships with relatives, friends, teammates, and with ourselves change. Nothing remains the same. Change occurs, whether we want it to or not and whether we like it or not, because we cannot remain the same. What we often forget is that, although change is automatic, success is not!

Perhaps because we tend to forget that change is an unstoppable, natural, and ongoing process of life, many of us are afraid of it. We need to acknowledge that life cannot evolve without change—it is what drives evolution. It is important to know and understand this law and to recognize that who and what you are now is not who and what you were, or who and what you are going to be. Recognize it, accept it, and then begin to actively participate in the process!

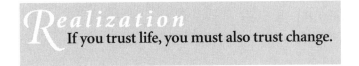

Realization
If you trust life, you must also trust change.

From Fear to Fun!

You have a choice, you can either choose your changes, or be controlled by them. Achieving the type of change you so badly desire will not happen by accident or just because you want it—you have to train for it. Life develops what it demands. Think about the idea that the majority of people fear change, but enjoy creating something new.

Question:
How would substituting the word *create* for the word *change* make our lives different?

Steer Your Own Course

You are the captain of the boat of your life in the fast-changing current of the sea of life. You can either steer your boat towards the destiny you choose, or you can let the fast-changing current of the sea sweep your boat along to wherever it is going. Choose to steer your own course; it will not happen by accident or just because you want it—rather, you will have to equip yourself with the life tools and skills and train yourself in how you use them. You need to know exactly where you are going and what you are doing, so that you will know what to do in the face of one of life's fast-approaching storms, or if you find yourself temporarily lost in the sea of life. It may help you to take your life in whatever direction you want it to go if you think of your mind as the rudder, your body as the boat, and your emotions as the sails. Some people get through life the difficult way, using only the oars of hard work, and find themselves being easily thrown off course by unseen undercurrents. Let's throw away the oars and find a better way by learning about our God-given gifts and putting them to use.

> *Realization*
> If you can appreciate the fact that all the cells of the body are renewed every seven years, you will begin to realize the possibilities of life.

Standing Still Is Not an Option

To adapt ourselves to the changes going on in the world, we need to constantly grow and improve. The people who struggle the most are those who are not willing or have decided not to participate in the process of their growth. Science tells us that stagnation does not exist in the Universe, so if we are not moving in one direction, towards our potential, then we are moving in the opposite direction. Remember the garden analogy used earlier, and that soil is alive and must and will bring forth! Whether roses are cultivated or weeds allowed to run wild is completely up to the gardener! If the rose does not bloom, we do not blame the seed!

We have all felt the Law of Momentum working in our life, either in one direction or another. People who want to stay where they are in life, but do not make any effort to improve themselves, will experience regression. In a world where change is a given, we must make an effort to grow, just to maintain our current level, so if we want to take our life to the next level, then an extra committed effort is necessary. To advance to the next level, the rate of growth within ourselves must be greater than the rate of change happening in the outside world. In today's fast-changing times, this demands a more committed and much-needed effort than ever before!

Realization
A person is old only when he or she no longer makes an effort to change. How true. Age has nothing to do with it!

Begin now to create and recondition yourself into the person you really desire to be. Otherwise, who you are now and who you will be in the future will remain unchanged; you will merely be a product of external desires and influences—from family, culture, society, and your environment. When we change our thinking and emotions, we change our life, and the whole world goes into transformation with us; we can no longer experience life the same way because we are no longer the same!

Realization
The condition of our total being determines how we influence the world and can ultimately change it!

Change and Acceptance

As technologically advanced as our society is today, we still can never make other people change, or change for them, because change has to come from within. Most of us have learned this the hard way through experiences within personal and professional relationships. It is truly amazing how much time and energy some of us put into trying to get others to change in order to suit our own idea of things. It is far more productive to invest our time and energy into raising our own consciousness and developing our gifts rather than attempting to change others. As we become more comfortable with ourselves, we will be able to accept others for who they are and appreciate and respect our differences.

> ## *Realization*
> The answer lies not in trying to change others, but in improving ourselves and making the world a better place.

We often resist change at first because it raises questions regarding our existing belief systems about how things work, not only for ourselves, but also for those around us. The ripple effect of change can easily be felt as resistance; many people find change threatening because it challenges them to look at themselves differently. Most of us have fallen into the trap of trying to please others and not stir the pot of old beliefs. Recognize that for every aspect of our life we have a belief system that we have incorporated into our self-image. If we take our current belief system into our next relationship, what kind of results will we get? As HUMANS IN TRAINING, we often hold on to our belief systems until a crisis—or even a series of crises—occurs in our life that forces us to change. Gradually, new information overwhelms the old belief systems until a new paradigm is formed.

Question:
If we are not meeting any obstacles, perhaps we are not challenging ourselves enough?

Resistance Is Futile

As we have all experienced in times of crises, tests, or trials, the Universe is very good at getting our attention and taking our life to the next level, with or without our permission. As HUMANS IN TRAINING, we can make this process easy or difficult by our willingness, or lack of it, to change and grow. If we are willing, then we need to develop the skill to listen to the messages that the Universe is constantly trying to send to us through life experiences. We also need to have the courage to take charge of our life and move it in the direction that the Universe has been trying to guide and take us, following the Law of Life towards our life purpose.

No matter what happens to us, no matter what circumstances we find ourselves in, the healthiest attitude is to accept all situations as they come. This acceptance frees us to make the most of every situation; when we resist, the situation persists because we deny ourselves the opportunity to learn and change. As we become skillful at accepting all circumstances as they enter our life, we learn to let go of all struggling, and when this happens, the struggle disappears and we change.

There are many examples of the Law of Change and the preparation process for change that is continually operating in our life.

---

*"The last ten years since being diagnosed with
Parkinson's have been the best of my life."*
—Michael J. Fox

Superman versus Super Man

The Law of Change and the process of preparation for change are reflected in the life of Christopher Reeve. The Superman movies were a phenomenon in the 1980s and no one suited the part, or could have played it, better than Christopher Reeve.

The world embraced four very successful Superman movies in which Christopher Reeve, the actor, personified that superhuman character that had been a comic book legend for decades. Not until years later would we see these same characteristics—strength, character, confidence, and invincibility—in Christopher Reeve, the real-life man, whom we now call a "super man."

Was Reeve, during these four movies, being prepared for his next role in real life? Reeve has made a greater impact on the world since his horse riding accident that left him a quadriplegic. What a perfect messenger he has been for us, demonstrating to the world the inner strength and spirit that lies within us all! How he has chosen to face adversity is an awesome example to everyone. He faces many trials on a daily basis, and if you hear him speak, you cannot help but be moved by his words.

Despite his many challenges, he travels the world sharing his story, raising awareness and money, and bringing scientific research to new levels, but more importantly, he gives hope to millions of others.

Are strength, belief, and determination greater than kryptonite? The HUMAN IN TRAINING behind the comic book character, Superman, is the "super man" who proves to us that they most definitely are.

Two of the many individuals who exemplify what it means to accept and rise above change are Terry Fox and Rick Hansen. Terry Fox, the Canadian who lost his leg to bone cancer in 1977 at the age of eighteen, began his Marathon of Hope across Canada in 1980, raising funds and awareness for cancer research by running with an artificial leg, an average of twenty-six miles per day. His run was cut short after 123 days, and he lost his battle to cancer a year later, but he became an inspiration to millions of people worldwide.

Rick Hansen, who suffered a spinal cord injury and became a paraplegic at the age of fifteen, also broke down barriers and changed people's perceptions. He completed his Man In Motion World Tour in 1987, wheeling 40,000 km around the world to raise awareness of the potential of people with disabilities. He continues today as a speaker, inspiring others to make a difference.

These young men showed the world what is possible for anyone who dreams big dreams and has the determination to see them through.

Another person who rose above her disability is the American author and lecturer, Helen Keller (1880–1968). At the age of nineteen months, she suffered an illness that left her both blind and deaf for life. When Helen was six, her parents hired a woman named Anne Sullivan to be her teacher. Although Helen never learned to speak well, she wrote several books, and with Anne as her "voice," she lectured worldwide raising money for the American Foundation for the Blind and campaigned tirelessly to improve the living and working conditions of blind people.

> *"Everyone who wishes to gain*
> *true knowledge must climb Hill Difficulty. . . .*
> *I slip back many times. I run against*
> *hidden obstacles. . . . Every struggle is a victory."*
> —Helen Keller

Realization The true alchemy in life occurs when we accept that every situation is there to serve us, our teammates, and society in some way. When we finally do, we free ourselves to participate fully in our adventure.

Glance Behind but Focus Ahead

All stages of growth come from having a desire for more than what we currently have. To achieve this, we set goals for ourselves; it is important for all-round success and happiness that these goals reflect growth on all levels— personal, professional, and spiritual. Working to achieve a set of goals motivates us to develop specific relationships, structures, and personal habits. Once these goals are achieved, these same relationships, structures, and habits lay the foundation for the next level of growth; however, they can also prevent it unless we let go of the old to make room for the new. We can become prisoners of what we believe to be success, sometimes for the rest of our life, if we lose our desire to change or if we keep holding on to old relationships, structures, and habits that no longer serve us on the next level, where we aspire to be.

Past and future do not really exist; they only exist in our minds. Yet they appear to be very real to many people who struggle because they are so focused on the past that they are not able to move beyond it. Others are so stressed out about what might happen in the future that they are not participating in the present. The present is the only time that really exists. The extent to which we live in the past or the future, rather than the present, makes all the difference in the world about the direction our life is taking. Whatever dominates an individual's present thoughts, feelings, decisions, and actions, determines the direction in which their life moves. Why is it that they make rearview mirrors in cars so small? So we can be aware of what is behind, learn from the past, yet remain focused on the here and now and on where we are going.

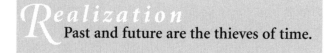
Realization
Past and future are the thieves of time.

The purpose of the present is to enjoy the process of constant growth and improvement while laying the foundation for even greater growth and development. The best news about the future is that it is never too late to change it, because the future is created in the eternal "here and now," moment by moment. Who has control of the present moment? We do, and each moment deserves our full attention. As HUMANS IN TRAINING, we can learn to live not just *in* the moment but *as* the moment, consciously creating. When we choose the future over the past, we enter a new stage of individual growth.

> *"It is only possible to live happily ever after on a moment-to-moment basis."*
> —Margaret Bonano

LIFE SKILL
Living in the present moment

Just as the participation of the mind is essential in organizing and nourishing the physical aspects of life, so the mind needs the physical body in order to maintain a calm presence, which is fundamental to all practices. The person living in the moment is in control of their thoughts; they are happy and highly successful.

LIFE SKILL
A powerful yet simple practice is to try and maintain presence in the body continuously throughout the day. Feel the body as whole. Using the body as an anchor for awareness will help the mind grow calmer and more focused.

> *"Yesterday is history,*
> *Tomorrow is a mystery,*
> *Today is a gift,*
> *That's why they call it the present!"*
> —Anonymous

One Step at a Time

The number-one reason why people are not doing as well as they know they could is negligence. Negligence and complacency are like an infection—if left unchecked in one area of our life, they will spread and eventually manifest themselves in all other areas.

I remember a conversation with a friend who went hiking with his wife. He told me that going up the mountain was a lot of hard work, frustrating at times, and took longer than expected. What kept them going was the fact that they could quite literally see the end in sight. They had a clear goal, which was to reach the top of the mountain. They took one step at a time and had each other for encouragement along the way. Interestingly, he said that going down the mountain had actually hurt more! The momentum of going down forced them to slow down, so they would not stumble and fall; as a result, they experienced a deep burning sensation in their leg muscles. Because they were not focusing on a goal, they experienced only pain and discomfort on the journey down the mountain.

Realization
It is the process that matters; it is the journey of creating, moment by moment.

Life can feel like a journey to the top of a mountain. Only you can decide if it is worth the effort to climb to the top of the mountain of life. Remember that change has its own momentum; we move either in one direction or another. If we stay focused on our goals and take life one step at a time, we will be aware of the momentum and keep it going in the right direction. Negligence and complacency help no one, especially not ourselves, to realize our dream and purpose, and furthermore, we cannot help anyone else if we do not continually improve our own life and take it to new levels.

"God helps those who help themselves."
—Benjamin Franklin

When we are not doing the things we know we should and could be doing, it causes us to feel guilty. Our guilt leads to a loss of self-respect, and with that comes a loss of self-confidence. When we lose self-confidence, we end up taking less action and therefore get fewer results. When we do not get the results we want, it is often reflected in our attitude and the spiral continues downward. As we have all experienced at one time or another, momentum is a very powerful force, one you should want to see working for you and not against you. In other words, the more you have—love, happiness, power, success—the more will be added to you; the less you have, the more will be taken away from you. The further down the hill you go, the more difficult it seems to be to get going in the other direction until, of course, the Universe gets your attention and you have no choice but to surrender to the Law of Life.

Be Who You Want to Be

Do not make the common mistake of comparing yourself to others or measuring yourself by yesterday's standards. Our capabilities are always growing and expanding, so we must not let yesterday's self-image linger in the shadows by hanging on to the belief that who and what we are now—our image of ourselves—is who and what we are always going to be.

> *Realization*
> Begin now to embrace and participate in change. Go from fear to fun! Our lives cannot improve without it.

"It's kind of fun to do the impossible."
—Walt Disney

The Process of Change

Look at the X and think of it as who and what you are now, and the Y as who and what you want to be.

$$X \rightarrow XY \rightarrow YX \rightarrow Y$$

It is a natural process to get from X to Y as long as you can clearly define both. X represents our current beliefs, habits, and consciousness, while Y represents our *ideal*, who and where we would like to be. This equation can apply specifically to one area of our life, or to our life as a whole. XY represents that all-important first step, when we begin to see some progress but our behavior is still predominantly the result of unconscious conditioning. As we continue along the journey, YX, the new behavior, is now taking over and we are seeing new and better results; however, under pressure or stress, we are still vulnerable to our old ways. The last step is the final transition, where we finally "get it"; the new consciousness has completely taken over and we can never imagine going backwards, regardless of life's tests or trials.

Tiger Woods is an example of someone who had a plan and grew into it. After his record-setting week at the 1997 Masters, he and his coach, Butch Harmon, chose to overhaul his swing. Most people have the idea that if something is not broken, it should not be changed. Why wait until it is broken? Would you have had the confidence or the vision to take such an action? In 1998, Tiger did not win any golf tournaments, yet felt inside that he was progressively improving and becoming a better player than ever before. Finally, after a year and a half of hard work, it all came together on the driving range. He hit a few shots exactly the way he wanted to and knew that he had finally succeeded in what he had initially set out to accomplish. Since then, we have seen the incredible results! Would you have persisted for a year and a half, especially with the pressure of the media and the whole world watching? How many people would have chosen to stick to their old and comfortable strategy—what used to work before for attaining quick and short-term results? Tiger Woods was smart enough to be looking down the long road, and he came up with a better plan. What about you?

We must not only understand this process, but also begin to see ourselves and live our life in terms of Y. The time is now to set ourselves free of the limiting beliefs and ideas of who we are. As long as we continue to see ourselves in terms of X, we cannot make the leap to Y.

Your Life Is No Accident

It is safe to say that everyone wants their life to improve; ironically, most do not want to work for it. They are either too complacent or they fear change, so they rationalize to themselves that their dreams will happen if "it is meant to be." As a result, they take no active role in the welfare of their own life. I do not know about you, but the first time I learned how to walk, talk, read, write, or skate, I was not very good at it. Does that mean it was not meant to be? I also remember how one day, when I was a teenager, my dad put a sign on my desk that read, "If it's going to be, it's up to me." This does not mean that we are all alone, or that we have to do everything by ourselves. Rather, we must simply do our part and have the faith to trust that the Universe will take care of the rest.

Question:

There are those who fear change and those who thrive on it. How do you see yourself?

Most people do not consciously create their life; theirs is a life left to chance rather than one governed by *intention* and *initiative*. The implications of not choosing to create your own life are huge; it can lead to a life of avoidance and fear of change. Begin now to seek change, create change, and take advantage of change, or else it will take advantage of you!

HOW to Change?

We have the opportunity to create the type of change we want by continually investing in ourselves. Our life represents a series of upward movements to higher levels of consciousness; it is a never-ending process of learning, growing, and creating.

Human development is an ongoing process; this process of change begins within us at the deepest level. Any change that does not originate here becomes obsolete in the long term. We all know the frustration of trying to maintain a change in our behavior, and yet we keep falling back into old habits. Trying to change behavior and habits without first changing the cause, which lies at the deepest level, is a long and frustrating battle, but a common experience for many people.

Weight problems are a challenge faced by many people in our society. Many can lose weight temporarily, yet have difficulty maintaining the results for the long term. Why is this such a problem? The answer is that they have not dealt with the root cause of their overweight condition—perhaps a lack of respect, appreciation, and love for themselves. Food can act as a temporary replacement for a much deeper need that is not being filled. It may also reflect a lack of understanding of the spiritual purpose of their life and of the body as their vehicle for spiritual growth. In their attempt to lose weight, most people concentrate only on changing their eating behavior and habits; they soon succumb and revert to their old ways because the root cause is still alive and has not been touched. I have yet to meet anyone who did not lose weight permanently when they worked on changing the root cause. Because of a greater understanding, they developed self-love and self-respect and began to exercise more and eat less and more healthfully. As long as we continue to search for a quick-fix solution, we are ignoring the cause.

Realization

For every physical or mental dis-ease, there is a corresponding spiritual disease. Miraculous results occur physically, mentally, and emotionally as we improve our spiritual health.

Consciousness versus Behavior

Consciousness is the cause and our behavior the effect. A shift in consciousness is necessary to better understand ourselves and the world around us and to advance to a higher level in the Game of Life. This shift can only occur when we raise our own level of consciousness, and as this happens, we automatically experience changes in our behavior that match the adjustments made within, at the level of consciousness. We must first go deeper in order to go higher! To advance to a higher level, we must first go deeper to the consciousness level and work with it before any tangible, long-lasting results can be witnessed. I find it contradictory when people speak about an inside-out solution to life with no mention of spirituality!

Any authentic change must always occur on the inner level first, eventually working and manifesting itself out to the outer level. As we begin to perceive and experience life differently, we experience self-transformation and the world transforms with us. Life does not change—we do!

Realization
Health, wealth, and love are all a matter of consciousness.

"Our awareness creates our reality in the moment; it is determined and directed through consciousness and presence."
—Jill Hewlett

"Keep Doing Whatever You're Doing"

I am very grateful for modern medicine. I would not be alive today if it were not for those doctors who performed the emergency brain surgery. However, I also found it frustrating that modern medicine acknowledges only the physical, when in fact, we are much more than that! The doctors could not explain what had happened to me, yet I knew the answer. At that time, I tried to explain to one doctor that the cause of my physical illness was emotional. I was holding in a lot of emotional energy, most of it negative, which had to be released somehow, and I was not doing the job. I explained that now I was attempting to take responsibility, that I was the cause of my own illness, that my inability to manage my emotional energy was the reason I nearly lost my life. The doctor looked at me as if he thought that maybe there was some brain damage after all!

My most recent visit to a neurosurgeon was even more interesting. The doctor came into the room with my original MRI results from thirteen years earlier and with the new ones. His advice was profound: "Keep doing whatever you're doing," and that was it. I told him I wanted more information than that, to which he politely responded that that was all the information he could give me. He told me that the diagnosis remained the same, and that he had no explanation for why I was still alive and asked me what I did for a living. I passionately explained to him that we are spiritual and creative beings and that these were the levels I had been working on. I told him how I was living my life "on purpose," spreading my message of INNER-POWER to the world as an author and professional speaker; I had too much to live for! My comment that I was both the cause and the cure of my illness drew a look I will never forget!

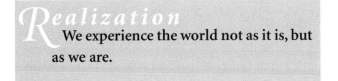

Realization We experience the world not as it is, but as we are.

It's Never Too Late

A married couple who compared notes after the first session at a HUMANS IN TRAINING course noticed that their notes were very different. My words were the same, but they had interpreted them differently. Instead of arguing over who was right, they recognized that they each perceived life through different lenses. Instead of trying to convince the other person to think like them, they decided to appreciate and learn from each other in order to broaden their own understanding. This man and woman, who had been married for thirty years, are now like newlyweds again! They made the connection that, according to their individual interpretations and definitions, when they argued, they were both right. Now they are asking intelligent questions, so they can better relate to the other person instead of making wrong assumptions. As HUMANS IN TRAINING, we can learn so much from each other!

Free Agent

Though every positive lifestyle change involves a period of discomfort, the rewards are in direct proportion to the efforts invested in achieving the desired change. We have two choices when it comes to change. First, we can refuse to recognize and keep defending our own weaknesses and old habits, which no longer serve us for our highest good, and as a result continue to make the same mistakes over and over. The second choice is to choose to commit to the challenging process of self-transformation by first recognizing and admitting that we need to change, and then gradually make the changes. Whether change feels easy or difficult depends upon where we put our focus and energy, whether it is on X or Y. If we choose to concentrate on Y, we must start to see ourselves as we would like to be and begin today to live in terms of Y.

FREE AGENT = FREE WILL

We are free to choose our own path; we have the power to do our own thinking and initiate our own actions. We can either choose to learn life's lessons quickly and move on to the next step, or we can choose to ignore the lessons and make the same mistakes over and over, suffering greater consequences each time. Reconditioning our consciousness means exercising free will guided by discrimination and energized willpower.

If you make up your mind to change, you can use your INNERPOWER to transform yourself. Willpower, an aspect of INNERPOWER, is the *instrument* of change. A strong will means strong conviction. In order to make progress in any aspect of our life, it is essential to develop our willpower and inner strength. The power of will springs from the inner Self; it infuses the mind and body with enthusiasm, courage, an increasing curiosity to know, and the energy to act!

Realization
In the power of self-control lies the seed of eternal freedom.

Getting Out of Our Own Way

In a seminar I was teaching, a gentleman stood up and said he was really getting frustrated with himself because he had been trying to quit smoking for seven years. I responded by telling him that maybe that was his problem, he had been trying for too long! I asked him whether he truly wanted to quit, or if he really enjoyed smoking. I questioned him because I figured that if he really liked smoking, he might just as well keep doing it and accept the consequences, and furthermore, if he was going to keep on doing it, he may as well enjoy it rather than feel guilty.

He assured me that he really did want to quit; however, he did not think that he had the willpower to do it. I asked him if he would give me his eyesight if I gave him five million dollars in return. He said, "No." I countered with an offer of five million for his lungs. Again, he refused. I said, "Your eyesight alone is worth more than money can buy, so if I offered you five million dollars to quit smoking right now, could you find the willpower to do it?" He assured me he could. I pointed out to him how this did not make any sense because smoking was jeopardizing his entire life, not only his eyesight. I added that if he gave up smoking, his health would improve, and that would mean he would have just won himself more than a lottery, because his health alone was worth more than any amount of money could buy. Once he gained this perspective, he was able to move to the stage where having a cigarette was no longer necessary or even an option, and he saw that all along he had had the willpower; he had only lacked the commitment to go all the way. Does this mean change is going to be easy? Of course not, but taking responsibility simply eliminates excuses. This man had to begin the process of reconditioning not only his mind but his body as well. He was kind enough to e-mail me several times to update me that he was still smoke-free.

Willpower is the spring for all our actions. To develop dynamic willpower, first make a list of the things you would like to do but think you cannot do. Look at your list and pick one "I would like to…" item and determine to never give up until you succeed. In the beginning, it is important to choose something simple that you would like to do or learn and determine to succeed in it. Be sure to choose something constructive and achievable, and then resolve to make success the only option. After you accomplish your goal, pick the next one on your list, and again, set your mind on achieving it. Eventually you will realize within your being that you can do and be whatever it is you want and that it was your very own mental limitations that prevented you from doing so earlier. As you exercise your willpower through the above procedure, it will get stronger, like a muscle, and become more dynamic, strengthening your confidence to tackle more challenging goals.

> *Realization*
> As long as there is life, there is an opportunity to change; as long as there is persistence and a deep desire, anyone can change!

As Ye Sow, So Shall Ye Reap

I used to find it amazing to think that even though life was a process of constant change, some people still never seemed to change. Then I figured it out: Of course, everything is always changing, but they are getting the same results time after time. If, year after year, I plant the same seeds, I can expect the same results. Each year the harvest will be the same, even though each year is different. It seems as if a lot of people want corn, but keep planting carrots, and then are not only disappointed but also surprised when the carrots show up. Each of us has the opportunity to sow whatever seeds we choose; this is a very powerful gift, so take advantage of it!

Question:
What seeds are you sowing?

As we raise our consciousness, we raise our standards of who we are. Our old ways of sowing seeds are no longer good enough when we discover new standards and better methods. This means we must challenge ourselves continually, knowing that if we do not take care to *create* our life, we will be forced to accept what life has created for us.

I once received a phone call from a participant in a seminar who jokingly said she wished she had never met me. She explained to me that she did not know this other level existed because she had not been aware of her purpose or the "Rules of the Game." However, she also recognized that to develop her INNERPOWER and begin the process of reconditioning her consciousness was a lot of hard work! Armed with a new reference point, she was excited about her future—to be a Player and participate fully in the Game of Life.

"People are always blaming their circumstances for what they are. I don't believe in circumstances. The people who get on in this world are the people who get up and look for circumstances they want, and, if they can't find them, make them."

—George Bernard Shaw

Questions:

What would have to happen, and what would you like your life to look like in one, three, and five years from today in order for you to feel happy about your progress and growth? What relationships do you need to develop? Do you recognize the relationship between happiness and growth?

The One True Constant

Einstein banished from the Universe every fixed reality except that of light—the only constant in a world of change. The velocity of light dominates the whole theory of relativity. In his famous equation, $E = mc^2$, Einstein proved that the energy in any particle of matter is equal to its mass multiplied by the square of the velocity of light.

Human standards of time and space are all dependent upon this one constant. The wonders of the motion picture, radio, television, and radar are also all based on the electromagnetic phenomenon of light—the essence of all creation.

Just as in the outside world, the only constant is the speed of light, so in the inside world, within each of us, the one true constant we can all count on is Spirit. Spirit manifests as the Life and Light Force within each of us, and it is what keeps us alive and interconnected. This Spirit is also the same lifeblood that circulates in the veins of all races across time and space. May we recognize this presence and give it full rein in our lives!

> *Realization*
> The universe is unfolding, whether we realize it or not. As part of the universe, we unfold with it.

"See the Good…
Think the Good…
Do the Good…
and only Good will come to you!"
—Edith Bruce

A World in Transition

- If you trust life, you must also trust change.
- A person is old only when he or she no longer makes an effort to change.
- Past and future are the thieves of time.
- It is the process that matters—the journey of creating, moment-by-moment.
- Health, wealth, and love are all a matter of consciousness.
- We experience the world not as it is, but as we are.
- In the power of self-control lies the seed of eternal freedom.
- As long as there is life, there is an opportunity to change.
- INNERPOWER must be cultivated.
- As part of the universe, we unfold with it.

"The purpose of life is a life of purpose."

—Robert Bryne

CHAPTER EIGHT

Our Purpose

Our purpose, as spiritual and creative beings, is spiritual growth—to learn to live as co-creators!—to recognize that we are all "in training" to progress to the Christ Consciousness as we become increasingly aware that this possibility exists within us and is attainable by all.

A Combination of Inner Work and Outer Activity

As we become aware of Universal Laws working on both the physical and spiritual planes, of the natural trend towards growth and evolution, as well as our inherent ability to know right from wrong, our destiny becomes very clear—as HUMANS IN TRAINING, we share a dual purpose. First, we must raise our consciousness above the duality of creation and perceive the Unity of our Creator. This is the universal path that every HUMAN IN TRAINING must travel, the path of spiritual discipline to that ultimate goal sought by truth-seekers throughout the ages—direct, personal experience with God. Second, we must lead a life of selfless service through perfect self-expression. As we surrender to our higher purpose, we experience real freedom, which is living out of the fullness and spontaneity of Spirit, without guarantees and with unlimited courage and wisdom.

> ## *Realization*
> Our highest purpose in life is to attain Self-realization, to know ourselves as spiritual beings.

A Marriage of Soul and Spirit

The inquiry into our Soul nature is the whole meaning of existence! We must realign ourselves with the deeper meaning of life and awaken to the infinite human and spiritual potential that lies within us. *INNERPOWER is God within*—it is our birthright and confirms what has been taught for thousands of years: *Everything we need we already have... we simply must learn how to use what has already been created within.* We are all God's children and must awaken from our Soul sleep, not only to God without, but also to God within. This is our true identity, meaning, and purpose.

> ## *Realization*
> Our true nature is Spirit, which transcends both body and mind.

The principal lesson that we are expected to learn is that we are the same One; we must learn to recognize the underlying unity of all life. As long as we view God as separate from ourselves, we will be trapped in a world of duality and will always need a mediator to know God. Because God is absolute, there can be no opposing power unless we create it and give it power ourselves. For example, the belief in and the fear of evil has come from a belief in two powers, but there is only one power—God. As we experience ourselves as separate from everything else, this sense of separation makes us insecure and afraid. If we are afraid, we are giving in to the belief in two powers instead of one. Each of us can gain great comfort in realizing that we are not alone or separate, but instead, part of a team. With this understanding, any life form would be seen as part of yourself. All life would be your life, supported by the spiritual body. The uniqueness of the human being consists in the ability to realize and know God. We should live our lives in alignment with the purpose for which we were created!

> *Realization*
> The inner meaning of life does not easily reveal itself; it must be searched for. Such a search is the journey!

Stepping Up to the Plate

Many people are unwilling to make progress on the spiritual journey because they do not want to face their fears or desires. We need to see how our demanding desires and blind fears, especially our fear of fear, are often the source of our own turmoil. As we progress spiritually, we begin to see how we are the primary and ultimate cause of our own pain. Inner doubts, fears, impulses, and unconscious motivations all create an imbalance that leads to mental and physical suffering. Disease indicates that we have been making an error in our lifestyle and thinking. It shows us that we must make changes if we are to live healthy, fuller lives. When we are sick, nature forces us to wake up to our transgressions from the natural laws. We must learn to use and value our difficulties and struggles as springboards in our spiritual evolution. We are witnessing this today in our world as individuals, companies, and countries are going through major "spring cleanings." Many "transitions" are now taking place as the speed of evolution increases and we prepare to transcend from the Age of Science into the Age of Consciousness.

The familiar expression, "It is darkest before the dawn," means that things often get worse just before they get better. This is because we are forced to face our old beliefs as they rise to the surface for the last time, so that they can be cleared to make room for the new. To break through old and limiting beliefs, we have to face them head-on. In today's world, this is highly evident as we see great progress, as well as great tragedy.

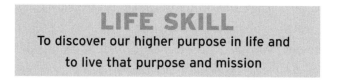

LIFE SKILL
To discover our higher purpose in life and
to live that purpose and mission

The Himalayan Musk Deer

I feel God must have a great sense of humor: We have been blessed with everything we need to fulfill our higher purpose and yet it is hidden in the last place we would ever think to look!

Musk is a valuable, extremely fragrant substance found in a sac under the skin of the abdomen of the male musk deer, an inhabitant of the highest Himalayan Mountains of Asia. The attractive odor of musk oozes from the navel of the musk deer when it reaches a certain age. The deer becomes excited by the odor and frisks about, sniffing under the trees, and searching everywhere, sometimes for many weeks, to find the source of the fragrance. Sometimes the deer grows angry and very restless when he is unable to find the source of the musk perfume, and he jumps to his death from the high cliffs into the valley, trying in a last desperate effort to reach the source of the rare fragrance. Then hunters find him and tear out the pouch of musk.

Many people act like the musk deer, looking for happiness everywhere outside of themselves—in play, in search of wealth or love—until they give up hope because they cannot find the real happiness that lies hidden within their own soul. If only we would turn inward, we would find the source of all true, lasting happiness existing right within the innermost silence of our own Soul.

A Greater Sense of Self

Somehow we have lost our awareness of who we are and how we should lead useful and aware lives. We expect others—our teammates, our children—to make us happy by behaving the way our ego desires. We want others to make us feel important, wise, and attractive. Some people spend years living together—expecting and demanding many things from each other—however, this has nothing to do with experiencing real love and walking on the true spiritual path. As long as we remain unaware of our spiritual identity, we are caught in the habits and patterns of the personality. Habits control us; we bounce whenever and wherever they bounce, and we react to the world with little capacity to choose our own actions. When we experience our true spiritual identity, the personality, with all its peaks and valleys, no longer exerts a claim. We transcend the dualistic nature of the physical world and experience an inner calm, a center that is secure and free of conflict. From this unattached center, we gradually resolve our inner conflicts and unfold the subtle potential of the deeper or superconscious mind.

To neglect the development of Self through dependence upon anything outside yourself is to weaken and underestimate your own nature. I love to use the statement, "The people who get the most out of life are the people who get the most out of themselves and the people around them." Simple enough? Why is it then that so many men and women go through their entire life without bothering to understand, experience, or harness the power they have within themselves? Remember how we discussed the difference between being a player and a spectator in the Game of Life? To so many people, happiness, love, and peace of mind are fleeting experiences at best; they are always "just around the corner"—a corner that never gets turned. The truth, however, is that we can have them all—happiness, love, peace of mind, abundance—all of them, here and now, always and forever. All we have to do is trust that they are already ours and live as if we already have them. To act like and to *be* that person now!

Each of us must learn to grab hold of life and begin to express from our own INNERPOWER with purposeful thoughts and actions. Each individual must know within that which is and that which is not in harmony with the Universal principle. Harmony is achieved as each person realizes their true identity and lives by Universal Law. Any disharmony in our essential nature, in our thoughts and feelings, is evidence that we are out of harmony with the natural order of things. The *secret to our progress* is to always approach every situation in such a manner as to preserve our inward sense of calm. When we reach the level of consciousness where all is harmony, we find harmony in all things, as well as in ourselves. Harmony is the principle that controls life; without it, life falls apart. This is true for any type of organization or structure that has interacting parts—nature as a whole, human relationships, or corporate business.

Realization
Harmony is the soul of any organization.

"Everything in the future will improve if you are making a spiritual effort now."
—Swami Sri Yukteswar

Your Most Important Investment

How is it that you and I can live in such a technological-ly advanced civilization and yet know and understand so little about the most important asset we have, ourselves? INNERPOWER recognizes that the single most important investment you and I can make in life is in ourselves— the only instrument we have with which to create our life, to contribute, and to make a difference in the world.

YOU are the investment! YOU are the most valu-able resource! The only asset you are guaranteed to keep and live with for your entire life—like it or not. Things, events, and people will come and go in your lifetime, but YOU will always be there. A true lifetime guarantee!

If you want to increase the rate of return on your most valuable resource, you must be willing to invest in yourself and do so intelligently, just as you would do with your money. Therefore, learn to invest your time and effort carefully and do all your homework, keeping in mind that you cannot get a big return if you do not invest wisely!

Question:

What is your life worth to you? Is it worth investing in? We are talking about your dreams, vision, relationships, career, and your INNERPOWER.

Realization
Your *security* in life lies in you, so bet on yourself!

The Twenty-Dollar Bill

A well-known speaker began his seminar by holding up a twenty-dollar bill. In the room of 200, he asked, "Who would like this twenty-dollar bill?" Hands started going up. He said, "I am going to give this twenty dollars to one of you, but first let me do this." He proceeded to crumple the bill up. He then asked, "Who still wants it?" Hands still went up. "Well," he replied, "what if I do this?" And he dropped it on the ground and started to grind it into the floor with his shoe. He picked it up, now all crumpled and dirty, "Now who still wants it?" The hands still went into the air. "My friends, you have all learned a vary valuable lesson. No matter what I did to the money, you still wanted it because it did not decrease in value. It was still worth twenty dollars. Many times in our lives, we are dropped, crumpled, and ground into the dirt by the decisions we make and the circumstances that come our way. We feel as though we are worthless. But no matter what has happened or what will happen, you will never lose your value. You are special—don't ever forget it! Never let yesterday's disappointments overshadow tomorrow's dreams."

Source unknown

Responsibility is Power

Accepting that you are responsible can certainly be difficult, especially if your life is not working out the way you would like it to. Life demands responsibility from you; if it does not come from you, then from whom? If you always wait for other people and circumstances to change in order for your life to change and improve, you could be in for a long and frustrating wait, along with an ever-increasing, crippling sense of helplessness. If you expect the world and other people to fulfill your dreams and desires so that you can become happy, you will only meet with disappointment. You have to take actions for your own life, and the right time to do it is always HERE and NOW, and not tomorrow or another place. So do not wait!

Realization
Responsibility is our ability to respond to our true needs.

It is impossible for anyone to find peace, happiness, and harmony as long as they are expecting others to do for them what they alone can and must do for themselves. No one can give us what we already have within, and no one can awaken in us what we ourselves refuse to express. INNERPOWER allows you to recognize that no one but you alone can express your own life, and no one but you alone can tell yourself how you must express it.

Taking responsibility for where we are now and participating fully and intentionally is what real life is all about. A life lived absentmindedly, without any intention, awareness, and responsibility, is like a ship without a rudder, drifting here and there along with the winds of change.

Question:

If you life is your story, what story are you telling?

No one can invest in you or for you as well as you can for yourself because no one but you yourself owns your body, your mind, and your spirit. In spite of this fundamental fact, people are often their own worst enemy. I have found it strange that so many people are embarrassed to read a self-help book or to take a self-improvement course. They are afraid of what other people might think or say. They wonder if it means they are weak, or that they have a problem. In any case, reading a self-help book or taking a self-improvement course does not mean any of the above; it only means that we are willing and curious students, eager to find greater meaning in life. There is never an end to how much you can learn or progress, for evolution is infinite.

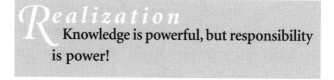

Realization
Knowledge is powerful, but responsibility is power!

I used to be surprised, when I offered my training program to a company, that it would always attract their top performers. The most successful people in the company were usually the first to sign up, while the people who needed it the most were either too skeptical or were unwilling to invest in themselves. At first, I thought it was because top performers are the ones who can best afford it. I quickly learned that this was not the case at all. The reason top performers are top performers is because they are always reinvesting in themselves to get to the next level, knowing it is not going to happen by accident. They understand the principle that to become better or earn more, they must learn more. It goes back to the point that people struggle through life not because of what they know, but because of what they do not know! Others have the attitude that if the company will not pay for the course, they'd rather not enroll, denying themselves the opportunity to improve their overall performance and quality of life. No wonder they continue to struggle!

Attitude

Most of us are aware of the importance of attitude in daily life. Our state of mind depends on it. A positive attitude engenders a positive state of mind and creates optimism and happiness, whereas a negative attitude engenders a negative state of mind, resulting in pessimism and depression. Where did we get our present attitude, and how can we develop a new one? INNERPOWER recognizes that our attitude is determined by our approach, and our approach is determined by our interpretation.

Realization
How we approach the world shapes
how we act and feel in it!

ATTITUDE = APPROACH = INTERPRETATION

How many successful people do you know who have a negative or bad attitude? My guess would be none. Our approach is very important because our attitude is born out of it. At every turn along our journey through life, we have the choice to approach it from either a positive or a negative perspective. Our choice is affected not only by the way we see and interpret ourselves, but also by the way we see and interpret the world as it happens around us. More importantly, the way we interpret ourselves, the world, or any experience is a reflection of our own level of consciousness. Our interpretation can often reveal to us who we are at that moment, and where and how we need to change. Recognize also that what we see in others through our own interpretation, we also find in ourselves. Have you noticed that when someone is criticizing another person, one often gets the impression that they are talking about themselves? Please be aware that our interpretation is not the *right* interpretation, it is simply an interpretation, often influenced by past or present circumstances. For example, we often see someone who gets a new job and is really excited about it, but as soon as they start the job, they find all sorts of faults and quickly begin to complain about it.

Questions:

Do you have the habit of pointing out or recognizing others' strengths or weaknesses?

Do these tend to be things that they have control over or do not have control over?

Do these tend to be the things that you also see or possess within yourself?

Of themselves, conditions and experiences are neither good nor bad, but neutral. Their effect on individuals is a reflection of the person's attitude, approach, and interpretation. For example, a roller-coaster ride can be fun or terrifying, depending on the interpretation of the individual.

It is our perspective and how we think about our circumstances that make all the difference. After offering my seminar to a group of financial consultants, a gentleman told me how badly he wanted to take the course but could not because of the timing. He said it was RRSP season, his busiest time; he was also studying for his financial consultant's certification, which had a high failure rate; and furthermore, he was married with three children. Right after he turned away, another person told me how anxious she was to take the course. She said the timing was perfect, it was her busiest RRSP season ever; she was also studying for her financial consultant's certification, which had a high failure rate; and she had a husband and three children to look after! Talk about attitude!

One of my favorite quotes embodies this lesson:
"Two men looked out of prison gates,
one saw mud, the other stars."
—Anonymous

Our purpose is to know ourselves as both spiritual and creative beings and to experience ourselves as such through our INNERPOWER. Let's choose to invest in our life and be an active player in the raising of a higher global consciousness! Do we not have an obligation, not only to ourselves, but also to our teammates and Coach, to improve our lives? Is not the purpose of life to grow, and so to evolve?

Question:

What has our past inability to effectively manage ourselves on all levels cost us?

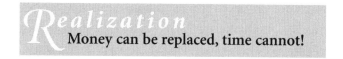

Realization
Money can be replaced, time cannot!

Honor Your Potential

It is my opinion that the most selfish thing we can do in life is to not develop our God-given talents and gifts. I believe it is the divine responsibility of each of us to develop our mental, emotional, and INNERPOWER; we are here to discover our purpose and our uniqueness. In finding and developing our gifts so that we can give them away, we play our role and do our part in raising the consciousness of the world.

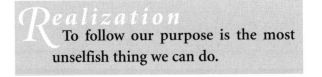

Realization
To follow our purpose is the most unselfish thing we can do.

In order to give something away, you must have it, and to have it, you must first develop it. The most important contribution you can make in your lifetime is you! Therefore, choose to develop and give away your gifts, personally, professionally, and spiritually.

Spiritual: Our connection and relationship with God.
Personal: Our relationship with ourselves and our teammates.
Professional: Our service through creative self-expression and unique ability.

Investing in yourself is the difference between being successful and not being successful. Investing can mean setting goals and creating a vision for your life—making a game plan. It can also mean taking time to be still and go within, to read, listen to tapes, attend a seminar with your teammates, or ask a mentor for help.

How does it feel inside when you know you are making a difference? I believe it is the inherent urge of everyone to want to contribute and make a difference with their life.

I recall being at a seminar with a group of very successful entrepreneurs. We were each asked to reflect on our life and write down what we most wanted to accomplish before the end of our life. Not one person in the group wished that they had made more money or built a bigger business; in fact, none of the answers had anything to do with business. What I found absolutely amazing was that every person had the identical response. What they wanted most of all to accomplish with their life was to make a difference! WOW!

If you want to reflect on your own contributions, try writing your own eulogy. You may be surprised at what you discover about the direction your life is taking!

Realization
The purpose of life for a Human In Training reveals itself in the privilege and opportunity of expressing the power within.

The Ultimate Win-Win

When we have the opportunity to do something that would allow us to become a better person—more powerful, understanding, loving, stronger, and productive—and we do not do it, we are not only cheating ourselves, but everyone around us. Ironically, whether we participate purposefully or not, we reap the return on our investment.

Investing in ourselves is the ultimate win-win for us, our families, our coworkers, our company, our society, and our world as a whole.

> *Realization*
> Every day, every moment, every thought, every action… is an investment in your future.

The same principle that applies to investing in oneself also applies to other areas. In business, an investment must be made in the development of people, the most important resource a company has! The key to building a successful organization is building and developing quality people. People build businesses. If we want to build a better business and get to the next level, we have to develop better people *first*. The expression that you are only as good as your people says it best; yet why are there so many companies that do not invest in the human element?

Technology and new skills are important, but they alone are not enough. Happy, balanced, and creative workers are more productive and create a much-improved atmosphere. Would you rather work hard for a company that shows a genuine interest in your overall well-being and quality of life, or for one that is indifferent except to the bottom line? How a company or a nation chooses to treat its people is reflected in how the people will treat and respect customers and each other.

> ## Realization
> The self-improving individual is the increasingly happy one.

However, we cannot wait or depend on others to invest in us first; we must do so ourselves. Life is too short and too important to wait for others to do for us what we can and should do for ourselves!

On the level of spirituality, this means studying and taking time for ourselves to get in touch with our deeper needs and make the important connection with our Creator.

"Give a man a fish and you
feed him for a day;
teach him how to fish and you
feed him for a lifetime."
—Lao-Tzu

It's Worth the Effort

Failure to take the time or to make the effort to better understand our world and ourselves is the number one reason for unhappiness. Each step that takes us up the mountain path of Soul evolution requires time and effort. Though every positive lifestyle change involves a period of discomfort, the rewards are in direct proportion to the discomfort and the effort invested to achieve the desired change. The great work for each one of us is to raise our personal perspective to such heights in consciousness that we become one with the whole. We must all ascend to the very highest in consciousness.

Realization
In Love, God is found in the world, and the world found in God!

SEEK
what the heart craves
what dreams reveal

FIND
what
matters

FACE
what lingers

EMBRACE
what fuels the soul

Source unknown

Our Purpose

- Our highest purpose in life is to attain Self-realization.
- Our true nature is Spirit, which transcends both body and mind.
- Stop looking outside for what can only be found within!
- *Harmony* is the soul of any organization.
- Your *security* in life lies in you, so bet on yourself!
- Responsibility is our ability to respond to our true needs.
- Knowledge is powerful, but responsibility is power!
- To follow our purpose is the most unselfish thing we can do.
- Every day is an investment in your future.
- The self-improving individual is the increasingly happy one.

"The road is better than the end."
—Cervantes

CHAPTER NINE

Enjoying the Journey

When our inner being is truly free, we find a wealth of treasure within ourselves—love, joy, and peace of mind. We can appreciate the beauty of life, taking each experience as it comes, opening our hearts to it and fully enjoying it. Realigning these qualities is the greatest freedom that can be gained.

Spiritual Mountaineering

Having read a lot of books, studied the lives of successful people, and taught the HUMANS IN TRAINING course, I have discovered that success means different things to different people. It has a different meaning and purpose to each individual. The dictionary defines success as the accumulation of material possessions or the attainment of a position of power or prestige. Although these can indicate success, are they necessarily the definition for everyone? If a person is successful financially but a poor parent or spouse, are they successful? On the other hand, if a person is a successful parent and spouse but cannot provide for their family, are they successful? If a person has all the above, but no sense of passion or purpose in their life or connection with God, are they successful? If we are not happy in our life, are we successful? Perhaps whether or not we are fulfilled is the true test of success.

My favorite analogy for reaching success is mountain climbing. Why do mountain climbers climb mountains? Their goal is to get to the top, agree? And what do they do once they get there? They come back down and find another mountain to climb. Is the next mountain easier or more challenging for them to climb? It is always more challenging. Why? It is all about the journey! It is all about overcoming obstacles, not avoiding them, and meeting and facing new challenges. That is the purpose and pleasure. As we climb the mountain of success in our own life, we see that no two paths are the same, and we see that our journey for meaning, purpose, and happiness began the day we were born.

The Path of Least Resistance

There are many paths to success, just as there are many ways to climb a mountain, or if we choose, to go around it. The different paths exist because we are all unique individuals, endowed with different personalities, tendencies, skills, or talents. In addition, individuals themselves are free to choose either the most direct way to success or the "normal" way, which is full of ups and downs— sometimes very painful downs that eventually lead to the final destination. The most direct and efficient way is always available for everyone, no matter where they are at present. However, this does mean that they have to take time to go within and find out what that way is, and then have the *courage* and *responsibility* to live it! There is no right or wrong path. There is only a deviating or a straight path, and although the climb may be difficult for some, the view from the top will always be spectacular for everyone once they reach the summit.

Once we stretch ourselves beyond what we thought we could do, beyond our self-imposed limitations, we can never go back to being the same person we were before, no matter how hard we might try. The new person that emerges from this process will always be a freer and stronger person. Yet why is it then that we tend to resist change and avoid failure? Should we not embrace both as essential parts of our journey up the mountain, knowing always that we can only get better in the end?

Realization
Every day a new journey begins! Every day is a new beginning.

Does Money Equal $uccess?

Although the majority of people think of money as the number-one indicator of success, when you really think about it, money does not buy the things to which we assign the highest value in life. Money does not buy true love, health, or happiness; create real self-confidence or a true identity; develop character; cement relationships; or, most importantly, money does not ensure peace of mind, which is what we are all after, is it not? Recognize that each of these assets is a property of the inner world and no amount of money can purchase them. So why is it that we spend so much time worrying about the outer world? Why is it that our society places such primary importance on outward appearances and material conditions? Do you feel the need to balance inner needs with outer demands in your life? You only need to look at all the advertising we are bombarded with on radio and television, in magazines and newspapers, and more, to realize how "out of balance" our society really is.

> *Realization*
> We are accustomed to noise and display, and yet the quiet but most powerful forces in the world and in ourselves go unnoticed!

INNERPOWER teaches us to achieve success from the inside out. When success is attained in this way, it is permanent and sustaining. We learn to go within for love, happiness, confidence, character, and health—mental, emotional, and physical. With each of these needs and qualities firmly in place, progress naturally takes place, sometimes at surprising speed, and we can actually enjoy the process. Therefore, wait no longer for success to come knocking at your door. Make an effort to reevaluate your whole life. Find out what area you need to change, and then change willingly and courageously. Life is not meant to be a struggle. Are you willing to give up all your inner resistance to achieve the highest level of success? Do not base your success on only material or physical achievements, for they are here today and gone tomorrow when death comes calling at your door. Base the highest level of your success on something eternal and lasting, something that you can take with you no matter where you are, even beyond the shore of death.

> *R*ealization
> Many people are unaware of their purpose and are working for things and situations that will only bring failure and disappointment.

Looking for Answers

Why is it that many people climb the mountain of success, only to arrive at the top still feeling unfulfilled? Were they climbing the wrong mountain, striving for a narrow definition of success that failed to fill the emptiness inside? If fame and power were the answer, when you reach these heights of success, why then are you left wondering why there is still something missing? If money were the answer, why are there people who have plenty of it and still feel lonely and miserable? I know people who have great financial wealth who are very happy, and I know others who are materially poor and are also happy. Interesting, is it not? This should teach us that real success has nothing to do with money; it is a choice that we alone and no one else can make for us. As Abraham Lincoln said, "Most people are as happy as they make up their minds to be." He was absolutely correct. Happiness is a *choice*, a decision that we make. There are people with excellent health who are unhappy, and there are those with highly "successful" careers who feel they have nothing. At the other extreme, there are people with barely any physical advantages, yet who are the most carefree and happy people on earth, and there are those with barely a career, such as part-time workers, who are happy and content with their life. Obviously, there is more here than meets the eye. To be happy, we should strive for good health, a well-balanced mind, the right work that allows us to express our creative uniqueness, a prosperous life of giving and receiving, a grateful heart, and, of course, wisdom and knowledge of God.

Realization
That which we are seeking is right within ourselves—the last place we may think to look!

Success Is in the Climb, Not at the Peak

Let me offer you a new description of success—one that you can use for the rest of your life. From this moment on, think of success as existing in the *effort* and not in the final outcome. As long as we try, we give ourselves a chance to grow and learn. As long as we do not try or do not do all the things we could do, we gain nothing, and furthermore, we lose self-respect and self-confidence. Success is only a matter of time as long as we persevere and never allow any doubts to affect our actions. We have all experienced, in one way or another, the miserable feeling when we did not give something our full attention and effort and later wished we had, for the experience would have served us well. When this happens, our progress is delayed, and we find ourselves having to learn later on what we could have learned earlier.

LIFE SKILL
Enjoying the journey of your
unique life unfolding

"It is better to travel hopefully than to arrive."
—Robert Lewis Stevenson

Then What?

An American businessman was at the pier of a small, coastal Mexican village when a small boat with just one fisherman docked. Inside the small boat were several large yellow fin tuna. The American complimented the Mexican on the quality of his fish and asked how long it took to catch them. The Mexican replied, "only a little while."

The American then asked why he didn't stay out longer and catch more fish. The Mexican said he had enough to support his family's immediate needs. The American then asked, "but what do you do with the rest of your time?"

The Mexican fisherman said, "I sleep late, fish a little, play with my children, take siesta with my wife, Maria, stroll into the village each evening, where I sip wine, and play guitar with my amigos. I have a full and busy life, señor."

The American scoffed, "I am a Harvard MBA graduate and could help you. You should spend more time fishing and, with the proceeds, buy a bigger boat. With the proceeds from the bigger boat, you could buy several boats. Eventually, you would have a fleet of fishing boats. Instead of selling your catch to a middleman, you would sell directly to the processor, eventually opening your own cannery. You would control the product, processing, and distribution. You would need to leave this small, coastal fishing village and move to Mexico City, then Los Angeles, and eventually New York City, where you would run your expanding enterprise."

The Mexican fisherman asked, "But señor, how long will all this take?"

The American replied, "Fifteen to twenty years."

"But what then, señor?"

The American laughed and said, "That's the best part. Then, at the right time, you would announce an IPO and sell your company stocks to the public and become very rich. You would make millions.

"Millions, señor? Then what?"

The American said, "Then you could retire and move to a small, coastal fishing village, where you could sleep late, fish a little, play with your kids, take siesta with your wife. In the evenings, you could stroll to the village, where you could sip wine and play your guitar with your amigos."

Source unknown

> *Realization*
> It is the very nature of our Soul to evolve through self-effort—the ultimate destiny for every one of us!

Life Deserves Our Full Attention

I like the way basketball coach John Wooden defined success in 1934: "Success equals peace of mind, which can be attained only through the self-satisfaction in knowing that we made the *effort* to become the best we are capable of becoming." Coach Wooden recognized that without peace of mind, no matter how much material wealth, fame, popularity, and power you possess in the world, in the eyes of your own Self you have nothing, and the only way to get it is through *right* effort—personal, professional, and spiritual. Please be aware that peace is not a state of mind that exists by itself. It can be attained only through focusing on that which causes peace within, such as success, love, silence, and healing. Peace of mind is most easily achieved when there is a complete absence of any emotional, mental, or physical turmoil, not only within you, but in your surroundings as well. Without peace of mind, success will always be an arm's length away. The basic ingredient for success is peace of mind; without it, we will always move restlessly through life, looking for someone or something else to make us feel whole. We will always want the other *thing*, yet when we get it, we discover that it is not what we want, and we end up feeling completely disillusioned.

Peace of mind that is dependent upon someone or something outside of you is superficial. Anything that depends on the outside is perishable, fleeting, and short-lived; anything obtained from the inside is imperishable and permanent. In truth, you are meant to realize and manifest all the very best—all the splendor, glory, and beauty of your true Self—but you first need to be at peace with all, including yourself, before the very best within can shine for all the world to see. How much do you value your peace of mind? What kind of effort are you prepared to give in order to attain it?

Realization
The effort must be total for the result to be meaningful!

Unity of Purpose and Effort

With this definition of success in mind, you understand that each of us is the only one who can know whether or not we are truly successful. We are the only ones who can know whether or not we have made the *effort* to make the most of what we have been given and of our circumstances. We can know the truth only when we learn to use our free will and reason in a constructive way, in harmony with Universal Law. Success lies within ourselves and not in the eyes of others. It is by our own efforts that we lift ourselves up and not by the efforts of others. Living vicariously through others is not only unproductive, but also destructive to our character and well-being. Therefore, rely on no one but your own Self, for all you need is already there, deep within you. You need only to take the time to look for it.

> *Realization*
> Our purpose lies in exercising the power that our position in the Universe presents—every person as their own determining factor.

The Failure Factor

When I began my study of successful people, I was amazed that at the end of their lives, even the most accomplished individuals wished that they had failed more often. What was it that they had not attempted because of fear of failure or self-doubt? Starting a new business? Professing love to someone when the opportunity presented itself, or before they passed away? They all wondered how much more they could have accomplished had they been willing to make failure an integral part of the success journey.

What kind of impact would it have on our young people if we were to teach them to enjoy the journey, that success is defined by the *quality* of their *effort* and by what they learn, not by the end result? What if they were to realize that it is impossible to succeed without some failures along the way? What if we were to show them that if they do not get the end result they want right away, it will still come eventually, and that it will come more quickly with greater effort and learning? If they were taught in this way, we would witness a great change in our young people's lives. Dreams would come alive. Success would then become the adventure itself!

Success would no longer be an option, simply a matter of time! Every great success was a work in progress up to the moment it became a success. Are you prepared to fail until you succeed? Are you willing to be a living example for our young people? They desperately need to see good role models in their lives. A good role model is someone who is not afraid to step into the unknown and pursue their dreams, someone who does not rely on their bank account or material possessions for security. Someone who bases their security solely on themselves, trusting always that the Universe will guide them and deliver all their needs, as long as they prepare and do their part.

> *Realization*
> Success and failure are interrelated; you cannot have one without the other.

The Journey Can Be both Exciting and Frustrating

In the art of gardening, there are setbacks and disappointments. Sometimes the seeds fail to grow in spite of being sown in what seemed to be fertile soil. Some seeds begin to sprout almost as soon as they are put in the ground, while others take their time.

INNERPOWER practice is very similar. Just when it appears as if progress is being made, something happens, which signals that there is a lot more effort to be made before any results will show. Because we are multidimensional beings, it is impossible for us not to have to deal with some obstacles along the way. It is of no use sowing seeds and hoping that just because the crop is badly needed, there will be no weeds when it rains and the slugs and other creatures will go elsewhere. These things are already present in the soil and have to be dealt with as they appear. In the pattern of life, they all have their function, and the gardener cooperates within this pattern without resentment and with understanding born of experience. Once INNERPOWER practice is begun, the waiting takes place unseen, and the seed that has been sown will surely come forth. A gardener needs to possess two essential qualities in order to cooperate with the ups and downs of nature—patience and self-control. Similarly, we must learn to cope with the ups and downs of our own nature and the obstacles with which life may challenge us along the journey.

Realization
It is not what we get, but who we become in the process, that brings value into our life and the lives of all those whom we have the privilege to touch.

"In all human affairs there are efforts and there are results, and the strength of the effort is the measure of the result."
—As a Man Thinketh

Success Is Not an Option!

My first experience trying to get a bank loan when I was ready to start a company took twenty-three banks to get it right! With each rejection, my confidence grew stronger, despite the obvious concerns of others. After each rejection, I refused to leave the bank manager's office until they told me what I had to do to improve my business plan, my presentation, and whatever else it would take to get the loan. Despite getting escorted out of three banks by security guards, I refused to give up. By the time I got to the twenty-third bank, my presentation and business plan were so good, I would have given myself the loan! From this example, you should see that success is not an option, only a matter of time, not to mention passion and commitment! Work on being a quick learner.

Failure as an Element of Success

Success depends on our efforts and on the constant demands we are willing to make on ourselves. In this way, life develops what it demands. Each of us must work on improving ourselves instead of wasting time comparing ourselves with others. We have to stop trying to be better than someone else, and never cease trying to be the very best we can be—getting better day by day. Thomas J. Watson, the founder of IBM, told one of his salesmen who had asked him for advice about doubling his sales to simply double his rate of failure! Some people never win because they are afraid of losing. People who avoid failure also avoid success because failure is the foundation of all success in any undertaking. Find out how you respond to failure. Does it inspire you or discourage you from trying again? Remember, no matter how many times you fail, pick yourself up and try again. Observe and learn from babies when they are learning how to walk. No matter how many times they fall, they pick themselves up and try again and again until they can walk without stumbling.

Visionaries

Love, Peace, and Happiness are desires of the heart of all humanity. They all have to be earned through honest and practical effort. Are we not all coming from a place in which the dreams of yesterday are but the realities of today? Who has accomplished anything outstanding who was not a so-called dreamer? Was not the eventual accomplishment first a dream or vision? All great souls are true to their vision; they never allow the nonbelief of others to influence them, and they never allow anything in life to block them from reaching their goal. They are willing to make sacrifices for their vision; they are true to it; they believe in it.

True success is the unity of purpose and effort, the ability and determination to carry out whatever we undertake. It seems that these days, many people do not want to do anything, yet they expect to see results. This is not only impractical, but also sad!

Sailing Over the Edge

I mentioned earlier that the world was once believed to be flat. As a result, people were restricted in their activities because they were fearful of going beyond certain limits in case they would fall off the edge of the earth. The idea seems completely silly now that we know the earth is round. It was round all the time, yet back then, people limited their activities as if the earth were actually flat! Adventurers who had other ideas about the earth dared to venture beyond those limitations and sailed to foreign seas and lands without any difficulty. It was simply a matter of "sailing" out beyond the limitations of opinions and finding that no limitations existed at all. While others were positive they would fail, the adventurers believed the chasm did not exist. We all have an adventurer within ourselves who is ever ready to explore life and dare to go where no one else has gone before. All we need is to learn to draw this person out into our life, for it is this part of ourselves that can ultimately help us to break free of the limitations of our ideas and mortal minds. Limitations are all illusions, just as the flat earth was an illusory idea.

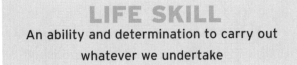

LIFE SKILL
An ability and determination to carry out
whatever we undertake

It Will Never Fly!

In mechanics, we produce something, then account for it afterwards. All attempts to analyze it first only indicate its impossibility. The airplane was never accepted as a possibility until it actually flew! This is true of every progressive step, even in our material advancement. How often do we let the "devil's advocate" talk us out of going for our dream? If you are not taking action to make your dreams come to life, then you will spend your life helping other people make their dreams come true. Some of the "wealthiest" places in the world are the cemeteries, filled with all the dead ideas and dreams that people were afraid to try because they might fail or because they were afraid of what other people would say.

A card that a friend sent me, which I keep in my *Humans In Training Journal,* says that the key to happiness is having dreams, and the key to success is making dreams come true. Isn't that great? As long as we have dreams, we have hopes; our hopes are what give us a reason for living. Human beings would not be alive if they did not have any reason for living. No matter how small or big the reason, we all have one. It is what keeps us alive and functional. Without a reason for living, people plunge into depression, and their life force withers away, allowing their spirit to fade, if not their body. Having dreams alone is not enough. Our dreams have to come true, so that we can feel good about our life. We have to be able to grow and expand freely without any restriction, to work towards a definite goal, to make a difference, and to serve in some way, in any capacity. A key to knowing if we are successful is when our actions are consistent and congruent with our desires and purpose. When we are inconsistent, the result is anger, frustration, inner turmoil, and resentment towards ourselves, which eventually spreads to others.

IDOL versus IDEAL

History has taught us the importance and value of having role models and mentors; however, it has also demonstrated the dangers of building idols. Yet why, as a society, do we continue to do so? It is much easier to build idols and put the responsibility on them than to take the responsibility to uncover the ideal and integrate it into our life—to *live* the ideal. Do you see how, as a society, we are constantly building idols, whether in sports, entertainment, business, politics, or even religion? We put the idol up on a pedestal, but as soon as the idol does not live up to our expectations, we become disillusioned and disappointed and often go searching for a new one. We read exaggerated biographies about individuals portrayed as if they were super human and never made mistakes. This causes many people to feel inferior and afraid to try new things, thinking they do not have what it takes. Rather than living their own ideal, they expect their idol to live it and they get caught up in the wrapping and miss out on the many gifts waiting to be uncovered within—INNERPOWER and inner peace. The solution here is to have no expectations of anyone, although you are absolutely encouraged to have high expectations of yourself. Instead of building the idol or relying on others for something you know you should be working out on your own, take ownership of your life. Stop being mentally complacent and take the responsibility to look inside yourself; there you will find the idol that you have often assigned to others.

> ## Realization
> As long as we build idols, we separate ourselves from each other and from God.

The habit of attributing certain powers to others and denying them for oneself is a practice that forever keeps people from achieving their own INNERPOWER. Refusing to live one's ideal in one's own life, yet expecting others to live it, is a habit that keeps many people from transforming their ideal into a reality.

> ## LIFE SKILL
> Idealize for ourselves that which we wish to bring forth from within.

Divine Guidance

To achieve your success, you must first discover what your passion is, what gets you excited and makes your heart leap with joy. This is an essential ingredient to an exciting and fulfilling adventure. You have a gift and a calling that you can only find within. Then you only have to trust that opportunities will make themselves available to you as you fulfill your passion. Every step and every stage in our life demands courage, faith, and determination. Thankfully, every day gives us opportunities to not only be daring and bold, but authentic as well.

When we give in to fear and self-doubt or let others decide our life for us, we create a void that nothing can fill. We may justify our decisions, but then we are only fooling ourselves and maybe those around us. The only solution here is to be true to yourself at all costs. A new adventure begins the moment you make this decision, and with that choice you will feel more alive than ever. All the burdens of imaginary fears, restrictions, and limitations that you have been carrying with you will be lifted off your shoulders. You will feel an awakening in life and consciousness.

Will there always be doubters and naysayers? You can count on it. Instead of letting the doubts of others discourage you, use them as motivators and ask yourself, "Do I want what these people have?" Being true to yourself is what is most important in developing INNER-POWER. When you are not being true to yourself, you experience emotional turmoil and disturbances within.

As a result, you obstruct the flow of life from unfolding the next step for you. You are never required to apologize to anyone in any situation for being yourself. In fact, people will love and appreciate you more for your ceaseless devotion to the truth—truth to Self in all circumstances. Weak people will have difficulties being true to themselves because they are too weak to stand up for their beliefs or dreams. If you think you are being true to yourself, and you do not have any doubters or anyone questioning your choices, perhaps you are not thinking big enough. To pursue your purpose and find your uniqueness is the most unselfish act you can do for yourself or anyone. As you do your part, you are contributing to the whole. It is the most precious gift you could ever offer to the world.

LIFE SKILL
The courage to speak and share your Truth—
to live without compromise!

"I went to the woods because I wanted to live deliberately. I wanted to live deep and suck out all the marrow of life . . . to put to rout all that was not life; and not, when I came to die, discover I had not lived."
—Henry David Thoreau

Commonalities of Success

In my experience I have found that successful men and women have several key characteristics in common.

1. ***An intense desire to improve.*** We must be in harmony with the movement of life, always trying to get to the next level in all areas of our lives. We must invest in ourselves through reading, attending seminars, coaching, or any other opportunity for learning and self-improvement. We must not be afraid to ask for help, and we must welcome feedback from others, whether it is positive or negative. We must learn not to be sensitive to criticism from others, yet welcome it with an analytical mind to determine if there is any truth to it. If the criticism proves to be true, we should immediately make a mental effort to correct ourselves. Everyone is our teacher.

2. ***Open-mindedness.*** In the course of spiritual growth, all our concepts, ideas, and beliefs must be investigated and reevaluated over and over again. We must remain open to the possibility that there are always better ways of doing things—that there is always more to learn. Recognize that any encounter we have with any person or situation has the *Soul* purpose of helping us to grow, to learn, to progress, or to find solutions to our self-made problems. We must look for a purpose within every experience, no matter how difficult it is. We cannot be afraid to try new ideas or take an informed and educated

risk. Remain humble enough to realize that the beginning of wisdom is when we realize how much we do not know. As HUMANS IN TRAINING, understand that learning is infinite.

3. ***Believe there is no such thing as failure, only lessons.*** We must view every failure as a lesson and extract the best out of every situation. We must train ourselves to see nothing but goodness coming out of every experience, no matter how strange or diffi-cult it may seem. We must step fearlessly into the unknown and always be ready to embrace anything sent our way. Without first-hand experience, we would not be able to grow in wisdom, strength, knowledge, and understanding. In childhood, in business, in sports, in all aspects of life we do not always get the results we hope for, yet that is how we naturally learn. To fully understand this principle, we must develop the habit of enjoying the challenge and no longer fearing failure.

4. ***Do not make excuses.*** We ourselves must do the inner work! We all have twenty-four hours in a day; it is how we choose to use this time most effectively, moving towards our goals and purpose that makes the difference. Successful people do not blame other people and circumstances, but accept full responsibility. They make time to get things done; they do not wait until they have the time to do it. Think about the expression, "If you want something done, give it to a busy person." Why? Because they will get the job done. I have certainly found this to be true in my experience.

Enjoying the Journey

To consciously create our life takes work, discipline, and willpower. It is a full-time job requiring single-mindedness and total dedication all the way. It is not something that you work on today and lay aside tomorrow. You may encounter many ups and downs on your way to success, yet never let the downs discourage you. Do not reject them. Love them just as much as you love the ups, for without one, you may not discover the other. As you train yourself to love and welcome both the ups and downs in your life equally, you will find that eventually there are neither ups nor downs. Everything just is. When you arrive at this stage, you will enjoy unending peace because finally you will have learned to transcend the pairs of opposites that exist within and outside of you; nothing can hurt you now or make you suffer.

Before you can arrive at this stage, you must first train your mind to always be positive and look for the best in everyone and everything. While you work your way up the ladder of success, remember also to take the time to stop and smell the flowers by the roadside. Do not live in a rush-filled life that you forget to take delight in. Live with your eyes really open. See and enjoy all the beauty that is around you—the grandeur of the sky, the sweet songs of the birds, the magnificent beauty of the snowflakes, and so much more. Go for a walk in nature and let it heal and uplift you. Remember to help all your teammates who are behind you and lost on the ladder of success. Help them in any way you can. If you cannot help them, bless them and give them your love. We all possess love within ourselves, so there is no excuse for anyone to say that they cannot help someone else who is in need of help. Love is the greatest healing power, the greatest help, and the greatest gift of all.

We can either make life work for us by consciously creating it, or we can just allow it to happen. The choice is always ours. To allow your life to just happen takes no work, discipline, or willpower; this is the easy way out. We are either doing one or the other. One brings with it growth and expansion, the other stagnation and death—death of anything, including love or happiness. What will you pick? The choice is yours—are the time and effort worth the results?

"If you do not change direction, you may end up where you are headed."
—Lao-Tzu

Instructions for Life

1. Take into account that great love and great achievements involve great risk.
2. When you lose, don't lose the lesson.
3. Follow the three R's: Respect for self, Respect for others, and Responsibility for all your actions.
4. Remember that not getting what you want is sometimes a wonderful stroke of luck.
5. Learn the rules so you know how to break them properly.
6. Don't let a little dispute injure a great friendship.
7. When you realize you've made a mistake, take immediate steps to correct it.
8. Spend some time alone every day.
9. Open your arms to change, but don't let go of your values.
10. Remember that silence is sometimes the best answer.
11. Live a good, honorable life. Then, when you get older and think back, you'll be able to enjoy it a second time.
12. A loving atmosphere in your home is the foundation for your life.
13. In disagreements with loved ones, deal only with the current situation. Don't bring up the past.
14. Share your knowledge. It's a way to achieve immortality.
15. Be gentle with the earth.

16. Once a year, go someplace you've never been before.
17. Remember that the best relationship is one in which your love for each other exceeds your need for each other.
18. Judge your success by what you had to give up in order to get it.
19. Approach love and cooking with reckless abandon.

~The Dalai Lama~

Enjoying the Journey

- To discover our meaning and purpose is the opportunity of a lifetime!
- Every day a new journey begins! Every day is a new beginning.
- Success is not only about the journey, but more importantly, about who we become along the way.
- That which we are seeking is right within ourselves.
- It is the very nature of our Soul to evolve through self-effort.
- The effort must be total for the result to be meaningful!
- Our purpose lies in *exercising* the power that our position in the Universe presents.
- Success and failure are interrelated; you cannot have one without the other.
- It is not what we get, but who we become in the process, that counts.
- As long as we build idols, we separate ourselves from each other and from God.

"Courage is daring to take that first step,
or a different path. It is the decision to
place your purpose above your fears."

—Unknown

CHAPTER TEN

The First Step

Ask and ye shall receive.
Seek and ye shall find.
Knock and the door shall be opened unto you.

Without Vision There Is No Direction

The time has come for you to take that all-important first step! It is time to create a clear vision now that you have the pieces of the puzzle. I would like to leave you with an effective tool—the HUMANS IN TRAINING Success Journal. When you put a puzzle together, you always have the picture on the box to look at while you put the pieces in their proper places. Imagine trying to put all the pieces together without a clear picture or vision to work with! Your Success Journal will provide you with that vision.

I believe this first step is essential in bringing the principles of the INNERPOWER approach described in this book into your life in a real and concrete way. As a fellow HUMAN IN TRAINING, I encourage and invite you to create your very own Success Journal.

Your journal will be a very personal collection of images and words that will communicate both to you and to the Universe who you are and in what direction you want to take your life as *co-creator*. It will document your goals, vision, identity, achievements, and sense of purpose. Your Success Journal will reflect your uniqueness and act as a reference point to manage your creative tools—your thoughts, feelings, words, and actions.

Redefining Your Self-Identity

Your Success Journal will be a tool for self-discovery. It will help you to determine what life has been preparing you for. It will help you to look beyond the wrapping and enable you to extract the gifts you hold within. The process of compiling your journal and working with it will help you to actively create a map or plan for your life that you will be able to follow with confidence.

There is no right or wrong way to create your journal, nor will it ever be finished. It will inspire change and evolve with you as you journey through life as a HUMAN IN TRAINING, reflecting who you are, where you have been, and where you are going. Your journal will be different from anyone else's journal, and anyone who sees it will immediately know the real you!

For practical purposes, you will need a three-ring binder to give you flexibility in adding and removing pages. Plastic sleeves are ideal. You will also need a couple of notebooks for daily insights, ideas, and affirmations.

Realization
Your Humans In Training Journal is not just a to-do list but a to-be list!

What Will Your Success Journal Include?

Take out those letters and photographs that you have saved and give them a special place. What about that poem that touches you to the core, or the newspaper article praising your achievement? Do not forget the first drawing your child made for you or the note from your teenager, friend, lover, or spouse. Create new documents. Let your imagination flow; let it tell you what to do and how to do it.

There are no rules here. Your journal could include inspirational quotations and images, stories, poems, and the HIT Lists from this book—things that you can read again when you need extra inspiration during those times when your road seems to be full of bumps.

My Success Journal includes a photograph that I created of my book cover years before it was published. I included a lifetime to-do list, as well as my "Vision and Purpose Statement." Create your future and let it be reflected in your journal. Include things that reflect and inspire your success—past, present, and future.

You might want to add things that reflect who you are. A photograph of yourself as a child, cards and letters from family, friends, and colleagues can help you to see yourself in all your various roles—as a mother, father, daughter, helpful friend, or appreciated colleague. Tributes for accomplishments, records of courses taken, certificates, and résumés can all act as pieces to the puzzle of who you are and what your passions and strengths are.

These discoveries can help you to leave the path of trying to be someone or achieve something that is not you. It can help you to focus on your path to personal success.

This journal is much more than a scrapbook; it is a working tool to inspire you to take the initiative in making your dreams and goals come alive. Use your notebook to write down your plans, ideas, goals, and inspirations; this will both sow the seeds for the right opportunities to emerge and motivate you towards taking action. If you habitually keep up your Success Journal, you will learn a lot about yourself. Your journal clearly defines who you are, what you stand for, and where you are going.

As part of my mental and emotional warm-up, I always begin each day by reviewing my journal. I carry it with me in my briefcase and refer to it for inspiration and conditioning and often add new ideas and insights.

Realization
The mind, heart, and Soul require daily inspiration!

We Are Goal-Seeking Mechanisms!

Appreciate the importance of setting your intent, focusing on the outcome, and being clear about what you want in life in order to make your dreams come true. By creating your HUMANS IN TRAINING Journal and writing down your vision, you are clearly communicating that you have chosen to be a player in the Game of Life. This decision alerts the part of the brain known as the reticular activating system (RAS) to join you in the play. The RAS awakens the brain to consciousness and keeps it alert. Think of it as the filtering system of the brain; it helps you to filter out distractions and direct your attention to certain things in your surroundings. The RAS is about the size of your little finger and extends from the central core of the brainstem to all parts of the cerebral cortex. It sorts and evaluates incoming data and sends the urgent information to the active part of the brain and what is not urgent to the subconscious. It alerts you to become aware of certain things in your environment. An example of this directing of your consciousness is when you might be thinking of purchasing a specific car and you begin to see that model everywhere, whereas you had not noticed it before. Once your Humans In Training Journal is a part of your daily life, your mind will begin working overtime to help you by alerting you to signs and signals that were there all along. You will also find that your mind will begin to send you all kinds of innovative and energizing new ideas for planning and expanding your ambitions.

Realization
Writing activates the reticular activating system.

As you review your Humans In Training Journal, write out your key goals and a clear purpose statement, think about them, and test your commitment to achieving your vision. A vividly imagined image with emotional content is as strong as the actual experience as far as our consciousness is concerned. By constantly feeding specific information to all levels of consciousness and cultivating it, you are providing the Universe with descriptions of the things you are requesting. Remember the phrase, "Ask and ye shall receive;" it is not, "Receive and ye shall ask"!

As you create your own personal Success Journal, your uniqueness will become more apparent, and it shall become your gift to the world. You will find that as you maintain it, your Journal will become an extremely powerful tool of self-discovery and motivation.

Three "P"s of Success

I believe in the principles of Preparation, Practice, and Persistence. They will guide you on your way to success and serve as preparation for HUMANS IN TRAINING books two and three, the continuation of our journey.

PREPARATION

In order to prepare to get what you want, you must first decide what it is that you want! A lot of people do not know exactly what it is that they want out of life, or they want many things and cannot decide.

Decide specifically what it is that you want for yourself and your life. Are you the type of person you want to be? What do you want to see happen in each area of your life? Have you set specific goals? Give yourself clear answers and write them down in your Success Journal, so that you can start focusing on them and conditioning yourself for what you want. Many people know what they do not want and keep focusing on that, so they end up attracting it into their life. You draw into your life what you hold within your mind. Remember the expression, "As you think, so you are." Therefore, use your journal to hold only the very best in your thoughts, and the best shall attract itself to you.

Try to make your goals as specific as possible. I also recommend that you have only one major goal in your life; make the achievement of this goal your top priority. My priority and life purpose are to serve, to spread the message of INNERPOWER and THE SCIENCE OF WHOLE-BEING CONDITIONING all over the world and to help people understand what it really means to be a HUMAN IN TRAINING. My purpose statement, which I write out every morning, reflects this commitment: To passionately inspire, educate, and love HUMANS IN TRAINING from ALL walks of life; to give them hope and assist them in achieving their own INNERPOWER. This statement reflects my *Soul* purpose, which both embraces and improves all areas of my life—personal, professional, and spiritual. I permit nothing and no one in my life to distract me from committing to my priority and life purpose. If your priorities are not clear, you may be going in different directions, which may cause you to feel unproductive and overwhelmed by your many goals. As a result, you will become emotionally and mentally stressed. To avoid all undue stress, prioritize your decisions based on your life purpose. Make sure that any decision you make does not force you to compromise your priority or self-integrity.

Our ability to trust circumstances and to meet our expectations is in direct proportion to our preparation for them. If we ask for success and prepare for failure, we will always get the results we have prepared for. Actively begin to prepare for what you have asked for, even if there is not the slightest sign of it in sight. Plan your life skillfully and meet opportunities fully prepared.

PRACTICE

All our dreams, hopes, and goals are useless unless followed by action. When you take action, you get results. Theoretical knowledge alone is not enough. You have to apply what you know by putting it into constant practice. This is the key to success. To harness your INNERPOWER, you must create and maintain your Success Journal and review it daily. This is one of the first steps to help you discover and recondition who you are and what you really want. It is a strange trait of human nature to prefer to think about doing something rather than to actually do it. Sometimes, we spend so much time "intellectualizing" about what we should be doing that we actually fool ourselves into thinking we have done it. Watch that you do not fall into this trap! Things do not get done all by themselves.

We have to be dynamic—transforming ideas and theories into reality. Doing the work is what actually makes success happen. Beginning is half the battle, so make a promise to yourself that you will at least begin each day by working with your Success Journal. You will find that it becomes enjoyable and you will feel good about yourself and begin to achieve the results. To gain proficiency at INNERPOWER, I cannot emphasize enough the importance of following all the instructions as outlined, every day, and whole-heartedly. If you do it only whenever you feel like it, you cannot expect to see any significant progress in your life. Put into practice both the easy and the difficult lessons that you learn, the tasks you enjoy and those you do not enjoy. Often what you do not enjoy is exactly what you need to work on to assure your final success. Make INNERPOWER practice the most important thing in your life, so that you would no more leave it out of your day than you would quit eating. A little bit of something is better than a lot of nothing.

After a keynote presentation I once gave, a lady made a comment about my Success Journal. She said that it was very impressive, but added that it looked like a lot of work. I asked her, compared to what, and would she rather live her whole life without a vision, without specifically communicating to the Universe and living as a co-creator? The alternative seemed like a lot more work to me!

PERSISTENCE

This is the single most important quality in developing INNERPOWER. What is it about persistence that guarantees those who have it an insurance policy against failure?

Persistence is the staying power that enables one to see a goal towards completion. Without it, people would tend to crumble at the slightest mishap. No matter what obstacles you may encounter, persistence allows you to simply forge ahead and ignore opposition. In any worthwhile achievement, you are going to find that there are many problems, difficulties, and hurdles to overcome. When life places a hurdle before you, you had better learn to become a hurdler! You had better persist until you clear it. Working with and gaining access to INNERPOWER is no different; if it were easy, we would already be using it to its fullest power. Accessing your INNERPOWER will force you to confront all your weaknesses, faults, fears, and doubts because they are precisely the culprits that prevent you from utilizing your INNERPOWER. INNERPOWER will compel you to be strong. It will send you tests and trials in order to increase your strength to its utmost capacity. The Universe will never send you any experience that you cannot handle. It knows exactly what you need and how much you can manage.

Achievement is attained when we realize that we should never give up at the first, second, or third defeat. We understand that if we persist, we will conquer all obstacles and finally achieve our goal.

There will always be times when things do not seem to be working out; listen to your intuition and stay true to your purpose and follow their guidance, even when you are not seeing results. Persist each and every day, not blindly but with the understanding that you know yourself, the way the Universe functions, the process, and the way the INNERPOWER approach works.

If you do not persist, you will never "get it"; if you do persist, it cannot be kept from you!

I have had frequent requests at my HUMANS IN TRAINING seminars for templates and help with creating the Success Journal. For further inspiration, I invite you to visit my website at *www.humansintraining.com*, where you can view not only my own personal Success Journal, but also inspirational letters and suggestions from your fellow HUMANS IN TRAINING. This will give you some ideas; you can download anything you like to get started. A special edition HUMANS IN TRAINING Success Journal binder is also available, specially made with an inspiring cover similar to this book's cover.

Enjoy the journey!

About the Author

Jay's path to self-discovery accelerated when, at the age of eighteen, he collapsed and was taken to hospital, where he remained unconscious for three days. At the time, he was pursuing a career as a hockey goaltender. He was diagnosed with a brain tumor and underwent emergency brain surgery. He lay in a coma for three days and was not expected to wake up. If he did, it was expected that he would suffer from permanent brain damage. He survived, without brain damage and with a life expectancy of only fifteen months. Fifteen years later, doctors cannot explain why he is still alive.

His brush with death gave Jay a sense of urgency to live life more fully. Armed with a new perspective and appreciation for life, he began his quest for answers about life's purpose, human potential, happiness, and peace of mind. When he was unable to find what he was looking for through traditional learning, he sought the answers elsewhere.

He studied the lives of successful people. He explored the limits of his physical and mental boundaries by sky-diving, bungee jumping from a hot air balloon, walking on burning coals, and more. He still did not feel fulfilled. He had not changed; his life had not changed. So he shifted his attention from his outer to his inner self in order to get to the *Soul* of the matter. He studied how the mind works and its relation to the physical and emotional aspects of human nature. He voraciously read everything he could find on human development and enrolled in personal training sessions throughout North America. Again unable to find the answers he was searching for, Jay decided to create a system to teach what he so desperately wanted to learn.

In the process, side effects of his earlier surgery changed his life once again. Occasional seizures and blackouts brought new challenges and opportunities. However, he approached each obstacle and challenge as an opportunity to more fully develop as a human being. He intensified his quest for understanding of how the mind, body, and emotions work together as one to affect personal health, success, and quality of life. He traveled through Europe and explored new cultures, different religions, and new perspectives on life.

Jay noticed that wherever he went, people were the same—hungry for inner peace. His travels brought him to an understanding of *how* the universe works and the importance and value of building a strong inner foundation, so that each of us can be a player in the Game of Life. He combined this understanding with his passionate desire to share his insights and experiences with others, to help them discover their unique purpose in life and learn to *create* the life they were designed to live.

The result is a journey of self-discovery Jay calls INNER-POWER—THE SCIENCE OF WHOLE-BEING CONDITIONING.

Join the Humans In Training Team!

Are you ready to be a Player in the Game of Life?

We would love to have you be a part of our team! Our purpose is to passionately inspire, educate, and love HUMANS IN TRAINING from *all* walks of life, to give them hope, and to assist them in achieving their own INNERPOWER.

We have created the HUMANS IN TRAINING Institute to reach out and raise awareness and understanding through teaching the SCIENCE OF WHOLE-BEING CONDITIONING in schools, corporations, associations, and religious communities.

The HIT Institute provides support, the opportunity to learn, and the forum to share your growth and experiences with like-minded souls as we travel together on our spiritual journeys.

To join our team, or for
information on how you can
request **Jay D. Allen** as a
Keynote Speaker or Seminar Leader,

please contact us at:

www.humansintraining.com
1-866-HIT-BOOK